Published by Tuttle Publishing, an imprint of Periplus Editions (HK) Ltd.

www.tuttlepublishing.com

Library of Congress Cataloging-in-Publication Data

Stern, Scott Wasserman.
Outside the box origami : a new generation of extraordinary folds / Scott Wasserman Stern. -- 1st ed.
p. cm.
ISBN 978-0-8048-4151-1 (hardcover)
1. Origami. I. Title.
TT870.S72745 2011
736'.982--dc22

2010037411

ISBN 978-0-8048-4151-1

Distributed by

North America, Latin America & Europe
Tuttle Publishing
364 Innovation Drive
North Clarendon,
VT 05759-9436 U.S.A.
Tel: 1 (802) 773-8930
Fax: 1 (802) 773-6993
info@tuttlepublishing.com
www.tuttlepublishing.com

Japan
Tuttle Publishing
Yaekari Building, 3rd Floor,
5-4-12 Osaki, Shinagawa-ku,
Tokyo 141 0032
Tel: (81) 3 5437-0171
Fax: (81) 3 5437-0755
sales@tuttle.co.jp
www.tuttle.co.jp

Asia Pacific
Berkeley Books Pte. Ltd.
61 Tai Seng Avenue #02-12,
Singapore 534167
Tel: (65) 6280-1330
Fax: (65) 6280-6290
inquiries@periplus.com.sg
www.periplus.com

First edition
15 14 13 12 11   10 9 8 7 6 5 4 3 2 1
Printed in Singapore

Photography by David Cooper

OUTSIDE THE BOX
ORIGAMI

A NEW GENERATION OF EXTRAORDINARY FOLDS

This book is dedicated to my parents:

To my father, who told me that my designs looked good,
even when they didn't (especially when they didn't), and
to my mother, who always helped and supported me,
without whom this book would never have become a reality.

OUTSIDE THE BOX
ORIGAMI

A NEW GENERATION OF EXTRAORDINARY FOLDS

Scott Wasserman Stern

TUTTLE Publishing

Tokyo | Rutland, Vermont | Singapore

CONTENTS

Paper Magic

INTRODUCTION

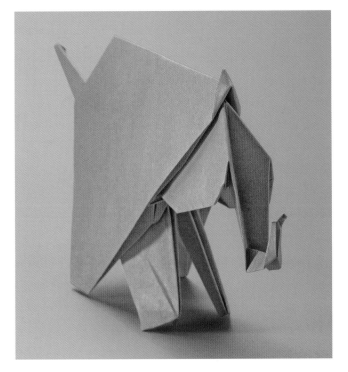

In 1922, an aging American magician published a book on origami and its uses in magic. This magician made the claim that many of the greatest magic tricks of the time—the disappearing ball, the repairing tear—all had roots in the manipulation of paper. This book did more than introduce a new generation of Westerners to the ancient Japanese art of origami. It showed how far origami had come in modern society—permeating even the highest echelons of American entertainment. After all, the book's title was *Houdini's Paper Magic*, and the aging magician was none other than Harry Houdini.

I was first introduced to origami when I was three years old. Masumai, a teacher at the preschool I attended, folded simple origami for the children; I was fascinated by the paper animals that took her minutes to make. Masumai taught me my first origami model: the simple camera.

After that, I began to attend the Origami Club of Pittsburgh (OCOP) on a semi-regular basis. I learned enthusiastically and started buying basic origami books without restraint.

Gradually, with the aid of the OCOP, the books that I bought, and several family members, I became much better at origami. When I was four years old, my family used to joke that if I was that capable then, imagine how good I would be once I learned how to read the directions! Over time, the books that I bought became more complex, the paper that I used was of higher quality, and the models that I folded started actually looking like the pictures did! As I grew older, my interest in origami grew as well. I developed into a stronger folder and I maintained my interest in origami. This interest developed into a passion, and I began to create my own models. My first model (the Star of David) was designed when I was six years old.

By the time I was fourteen, I had created about thirty of my own models, and I was proficient at many facets of origami. I owned books by some of the most eminent origami folders of the past century, and I enjoyed folding their work.

For many years, my parents had been encouraging me to diagram my origami models, but I had no idea how. But through a class at school and the assistance of my twin brother Eric, I learned how to use Adobe Illustrator, and I began diagramming my own models.

My models include such disparate creations as a ghost, a family of birds, and a snowflake. "When pigs fly!" you may say. Well, yes, I have a flying pig model as well. "That certainly sounds 'outside the box,'" you may say. Yes, I have that model too.

All of the models are made from square sheets of paper, and, as pure origami, contain absolutely no cutting or gluing. Even the modular origami in this book, creations made from more than one piece of paper, are connected entirely with paper locks.

It took several years and more than 1,500 hours of work, but I finally produced a book that I believe shows my

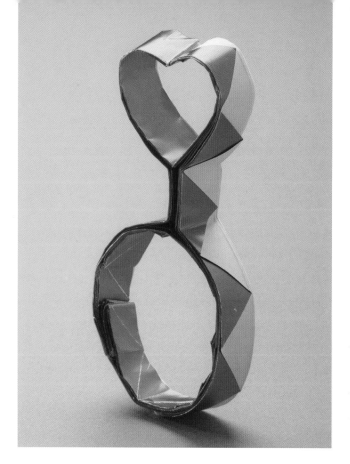

finest twenty models to date. I thoroughly hope that you enjoy this book and learn to love origami, as I do.

My interest in and eventual aptitude for origami were by no means the results of any inherent ability. I became talented at folding paper because I was exposed to it quite early and I had a very supportive family. My aunt is very good at origami, my mother learned with me, and my other family members responded to my folding with positive encouragement.

I was accompanied to meetings of the Origami Club of Pittsburgh long before I was old enough to attend on my own. My mother acquiesced to taking me to the National Origami Convention in New York not just once, but five times to date!

History is probably my favorite subject in school, so I believe that it is worthwhile to pass along a little bit about the history of origami. It is a common misconception that origami was created in Japan: it was actually invented in ancient China.

It is believed that origami was created shortly after the invention of paper around 100 CE. Origami spread to Japan about 500 years later and became quite popular.

European traders learned origami from the Japanese and brought it back to Europe. Westerners viewed origami with interest and it gradually gained popularity in Europe and eventually America.

Origami has evolved considerably over time. While squares have nearly always been used, the complexity of origami has increased. Over the last couple decades in particular, origami has become far more advanced.

Much of this change is the result of the influence of mathematics on origami. Many famous origami artists use math to design truly incredible origami models. However, I favor a different, more holistic approach. Instead of thinking of what my models will look like ahead of time, I prefer to fold and just see what happens. This may be less professional and less precise, and it may produce the eclectic mix of models displayed in this book, but I do it because it is much more fun.

I am a strong believer in the idea that anyone can learn origami—you don't have to be inherently talented. Origami is fun, relaxing, stimulating, and interesting; but, above all, it's quite easy to learn. Harry Houdini would agree: origami is truly magical!

ORIGAMI BASICS

VALLEY FOLD

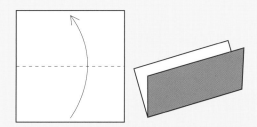

Fold the paper, forming a valley-like depression.

MOUNTAIN FOLD

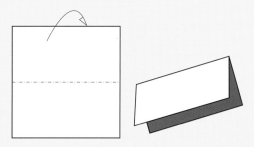

Fold the paper, forming a mountain-like protrusion.

FOLD AND UNFOLD

Fold the paper, forming a crease. Once the crease is complete, unfold the paper back to its original position.

SINK FOLD

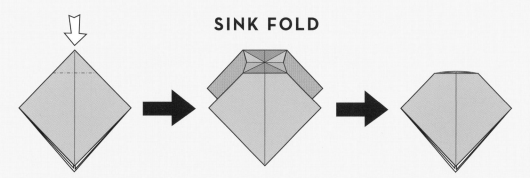

Open the paper and invert the tip, pressing it down into the model. As you are pressing the tip down, reverse the creases surrounding the tip, forming a square of mountain folds.

SQUASH FOLD

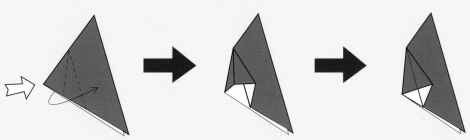

Open up one corner of the paper, swinging what was formerly a creased edge over and pressing it down.

PLEAT FOLD

Valley fold the top of tip down to a given point.
Then fold the tip back up to a point slightly lower than the original position.

REVERSE FOLD

Spread the top of the model and reverse the creases, mountain folding the top corner down and in.
Collapse the model while pulling the reversed corner down.

RABBIT EAR FOLD

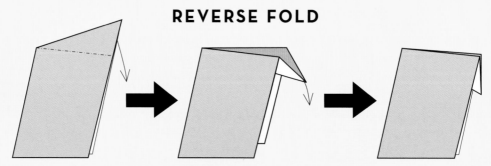

Collapse one side, so that the left edges will lie even with the center crease. To do this, make two valley creases; at the
point at which they meet, make another valley crease up to a corner of the paper. The crease should thus collapse.

PETAL FOLD

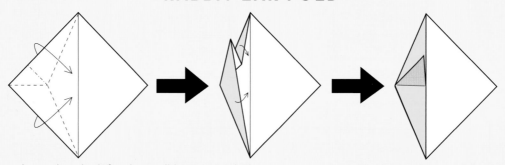

Bring the two sides into the center while swinging the bottom of the colored flap up, forming
a point in the center of the flap. The left and right sides will now lie even with the center.

REVIEW OF IMPORTANT SYMBOLS

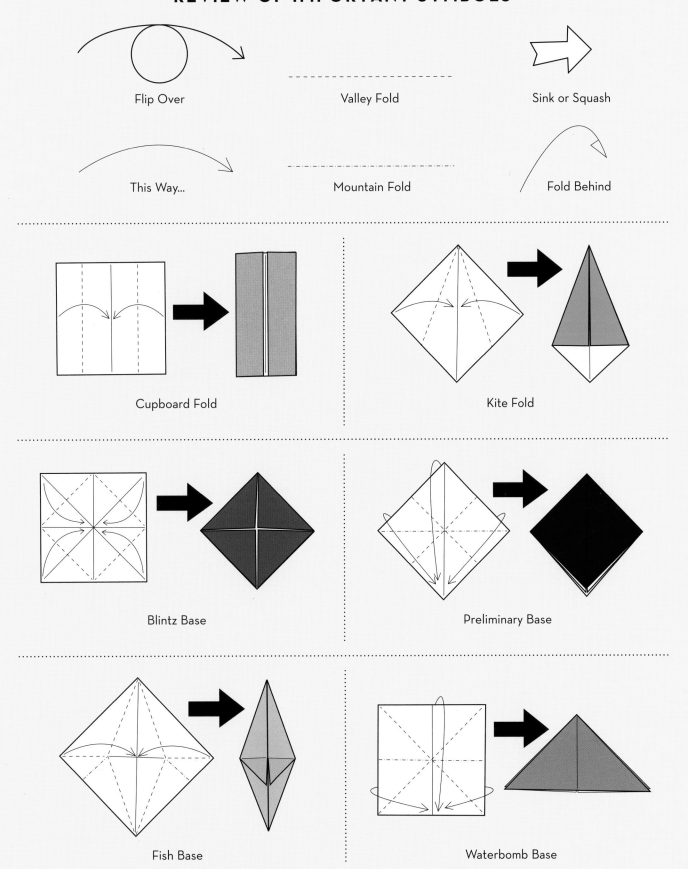

Flip Over

Valley Fold

Sink or Squash

This Way...

Mountain Fold

Fold Behind

Cupboard Fold

Kite Fold

Blintz Base

Preliminary Base

Fish Base

Waterbomb Base

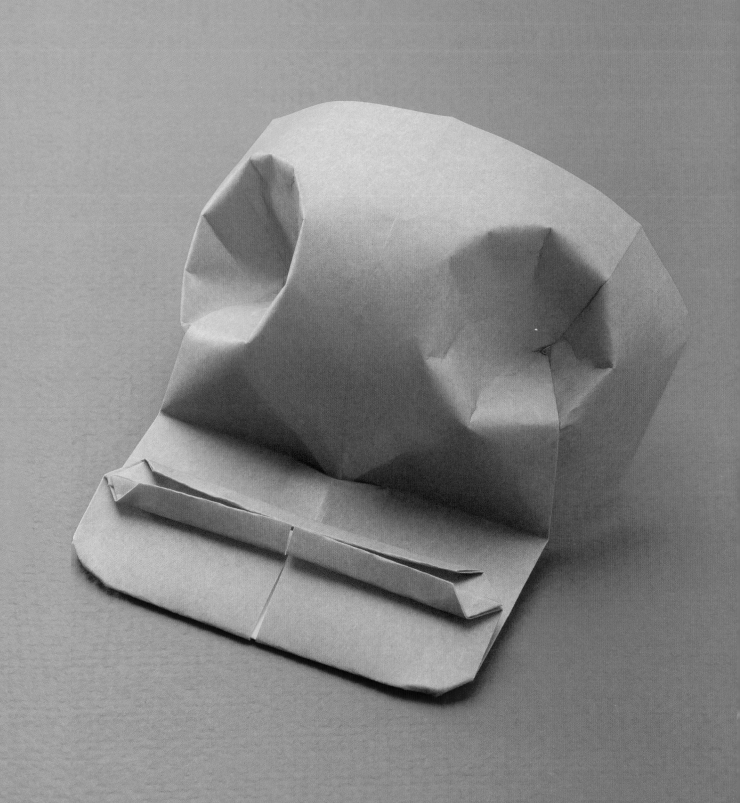

Part I

SIMPLE FOLDS

STAR OF DAVID

I designed this model when I was six years old, while at camp. It was the first model I ever created, and it was, without a doubt, an accident. I just did some random folds, and for a reason that I do not now recall, recreated it five more times and realized that they fit together. Though some origami creators design their models mathematically or with great forethought and care, I prefer this "let's just do random folds and see what happens" method. This method requires more paper and more time, though it certainly makes it much more fun when you find something worth replicating.

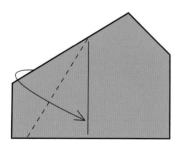

1 Recommended paper: six 6-inch squares. Valley fold the left corner in so that it lies even with the center crease.

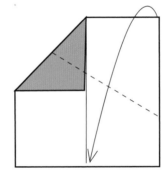

2 Valley fold the right corner down to the bottom of the center crease.

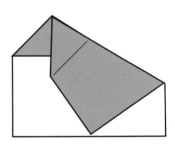

3 Flip the model over.

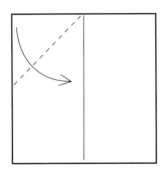

4 Valley fold the top left edge into the center.

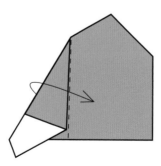

5 Valley fold the left flap across the center crease.

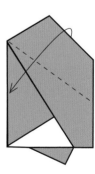

6 Valley fold the top right side down so that the top left side lies even with the left vertical side.

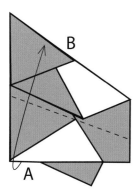
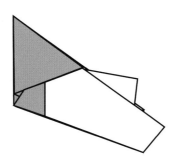
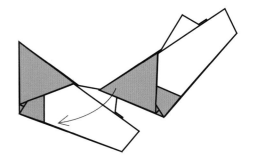

7 Valley fold side A up, tucking it into the pocket so that it lies even with side B.

8 The completed module!

9 To connect the units, insert one unit into a pocket of another, so that the bottom colored edge of one unit lies even with the bottom white edge of another.

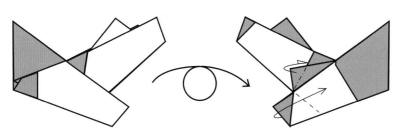
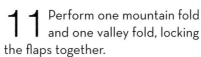
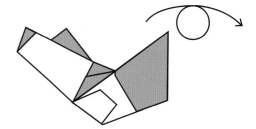

10 Flip the model over.

11 Perform one mountain fold and one valley fold, locking the flaps together.

12 Flip the model back over.

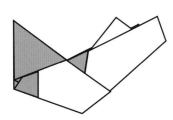

13 Repeat the connection process on the other four units (six in total).

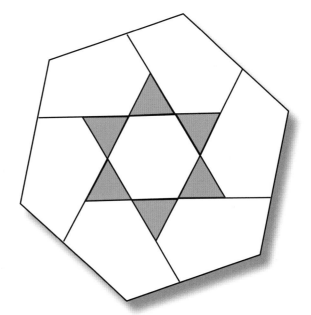

The completed model!

STAR RING

I designed this model quite by accident one day, while I was attempting to study for an exam. I was having trouble with science and I got a little bit distracted and—voila! Amazingly, these units fit together in a quite satisfying way. What I like most about this model is its intricate design that is only seen when you connect the units. Alone, even if you knew these units made a ring, it would be difficult to predict the appearance of the beautiful star on the inside.

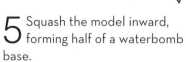

1 Recommended paper: eight 6-inch squares. Valley fold the bottom flap up to the center, doing half of a cupboard fold.

2 Flip the model over.

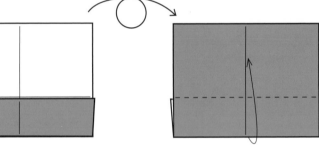

3 Valley fold the bottom flap up along the central crease.

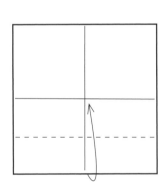

4 Mountain fold the model in half.

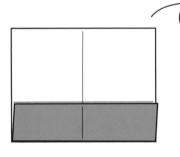

· 90°

5 Squash the model inward, forming half of a waterbomb base.

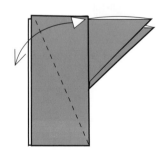

6 Valley fold the flap down from the top left corner to the bottom. Unfold. Repeat behind.

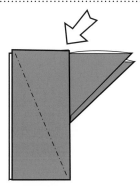

7 Inside reverse fold the flap using the crease you made in step 6. Repeat behind.

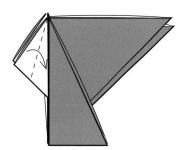

8 Valley fold the flap down, so that it lies even with the colored edge. Repeat behind.

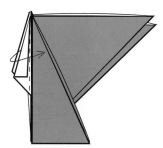

9 Valley fold the flap, so that it lies under the colored edge. Repeat behind.

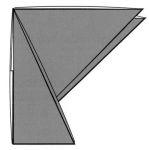

10 The completed module!

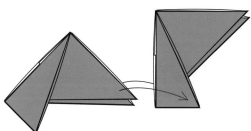

11 Put the two triangular flaps of one unit into the two side pockets of another.

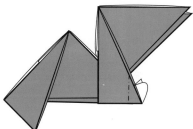

12 Mountain fold the whole pocket over into itself.

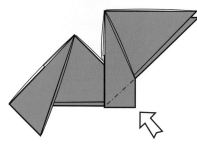

13 Perform an inside reverse fold on the pocket, squashing it into itself. This is the complete connection process of two units.

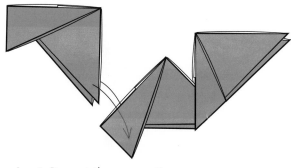

14 Repeat the connection process with another six units. The complete model takes eight units.

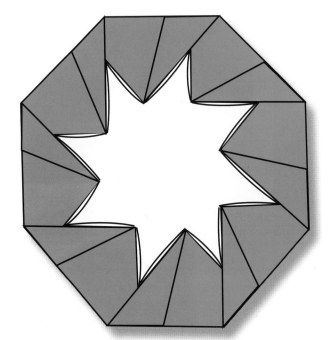

The completed model!

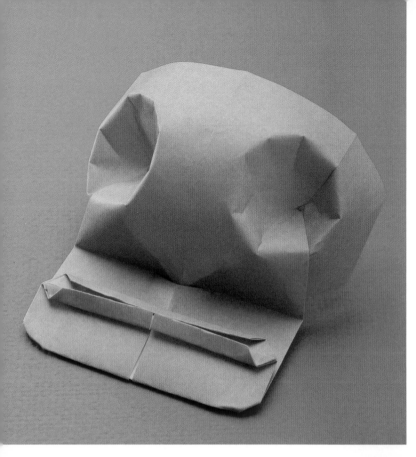

SKULL

This skull model was designed while I was experimenting with three-dimensional sink folds. It is very simple in design and equally simple to fold, but if the folder is not careful, the eyes or nose could look distorted. Nevertheless, this is a refreshingly simple model, but one that does not lose its integrity in spite of its short folding process. And, since it is based on a cupboard fold, this model can be done using any sized rectangle; my instructions, however, are based upon using a square (my favorite method).

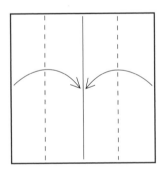

1 Recommended paper: a 6-inch square. Cupboard fold two sides into the center.

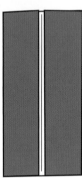

2 Flip the model over.

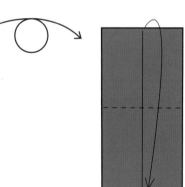

3 Valley fold the top of the model down to the bottom.

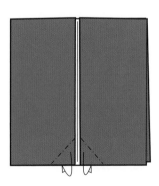

4 Mountain fold the bottom corners of the central flaps into themselves.

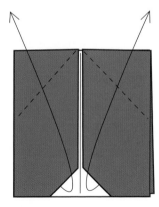

5 Make a partial squash fold on both central flaps, making as few permanent creases as possible. This brings the center edges to lie even with the top. The model will not lie flat.

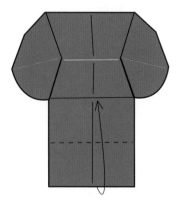

6 Valley fold the bottom up to the central crease.

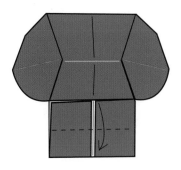

7 Valley fold the flap down so that it lies even with the bottom of the model.

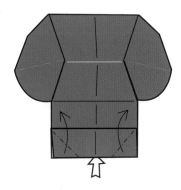

8 Squash the flap back up.

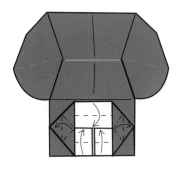

9 Petal fold the top and bottom of the flaps together, at the center.

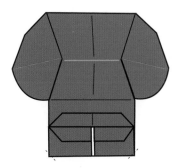

10 Inside reverse fold and shape with fingers to round the corners of the jaw.

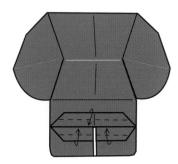

11 Valley fold the top and bottom of the mouth into the center.

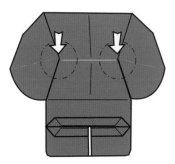

12 Perform a partial closed sink fold on where the eyes will be. Do not flatten the model, or crease too sharply.

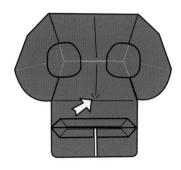

13 Make a small pinch to form the nose.

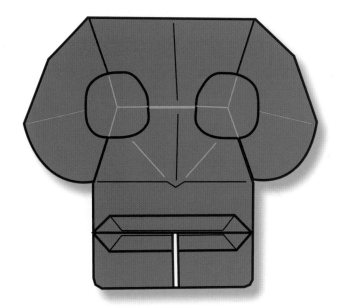

The completed model!

SIMPLE WREATH

This model was named the "simple" wreath not be-cause it is my simplest model; on the contrary, it has perhaps the most complicated connection process of any of my models. However, it looks simple, and its aesthetic appeal is undeniable. If you want a different effect, fold each module out of a different color sheet of paper and then connect them.

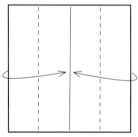 1 Recommended paper: eight 6-inch squares. Valley fold the two sides into the center, performing a cupboard fold.

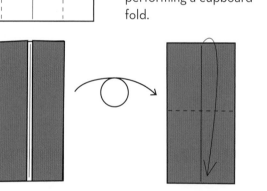

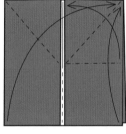

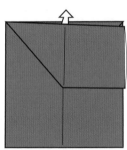

2 Flip the model over.

3 Valley fold the top of the model down to the bottom.

4 Squash the top half of the model up.

5 Pull out some paper from the flap.

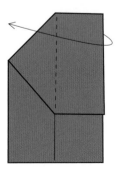

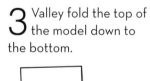

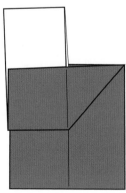

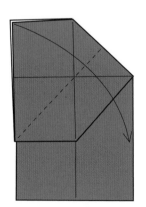

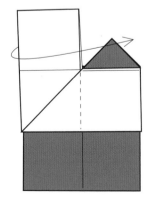

6 Valley fold the flap, swinging it over.

7 Repeat step 5 on this side of the flap.

8 Valley fold the flap, so that the side edge lies even with the base of the flap.

9 Valley fold the flap, swinging it over.

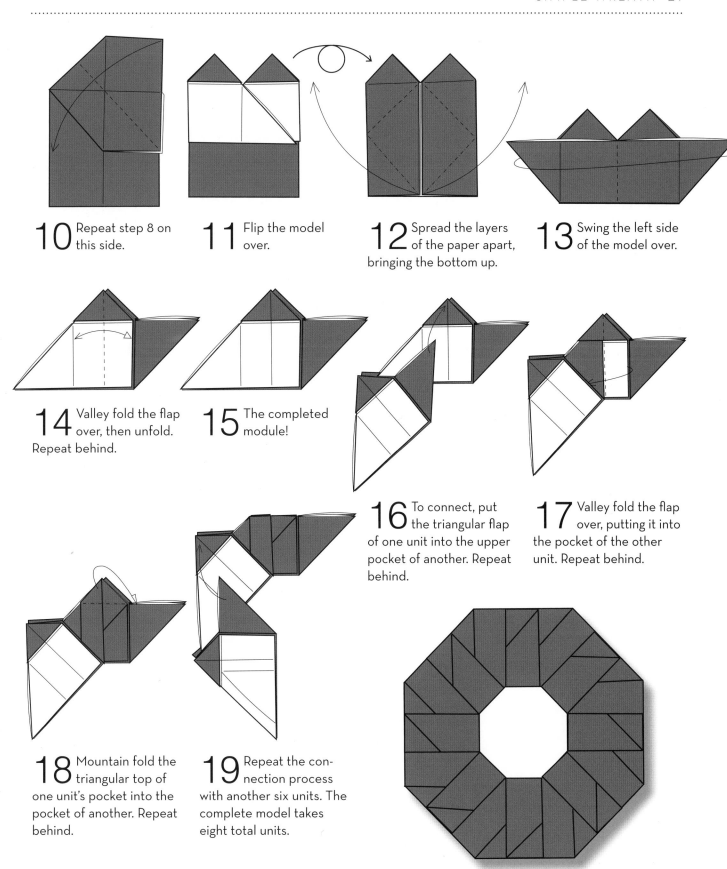

10 Repeat step 8 on this side.

11 Flip the model over.

12 Spread the layers of the paper apart, bringing the bottom up.

13 Swing the left side of the model over.

14 Valley fold the flap over, then unfold. Repeat behind.

15 The completed module!

16 To connect, put the triangular flap of one unit into the upper pocket of another. Repeat behind.

17 Valley fold the flap over, putting it into the pocket of the other unit. Repeat behind.

18 Mountain fold the triangular top of one unit's pocket into the pocket of another. Repeat behind.

19 Repeat the connection process with another six units. The complete model takes eight total units.

The completed model!

STARBURST

This was the first three-dimensional model that I designed. It was designed while I was watching television, and it was made completely by accident. Two modules fit into each other so well that I decided to make four more of them to complete the model! The process is quite simple in theory: each module has two flaps perpendicular to two pockets. The colors alternate, because of the color change done on the first step. Although this model is relatively simple, it requires a certain degree of precision to fit the modules together.

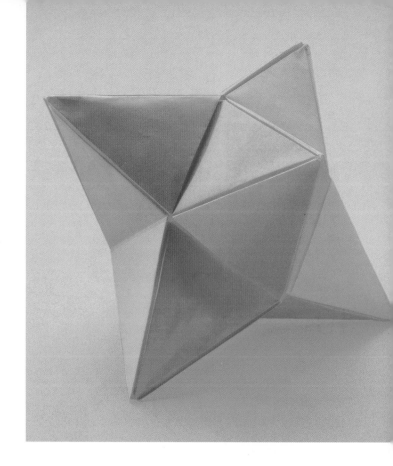

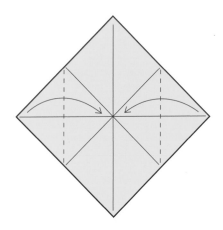

1 Recommended paper: six 6-inch squares. Start color side up. Valley fold two of the corners into the center.

2 Flip the model over.

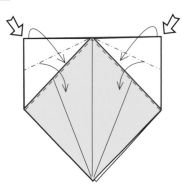

5 Squash the two corners over, so that what was formerly the edge of the white triangles now lies even with where you valley fold.

3 Make four valley folds, creasing the four diagonal sides in to the center and then folding, stopping at the diagonal creases, as shown. Then unfold.

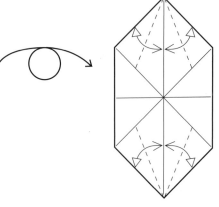

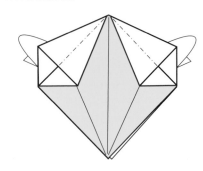

6 Mountain fold the top of the white flaps around to the back, along the middle.

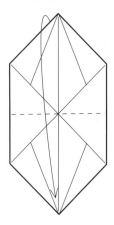

4 Valley fold the model in half.

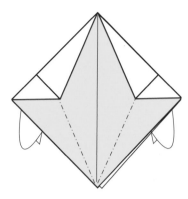

7 Mountain fold the raw edges inside and under along the creases you made in step 3. Repeat behind.

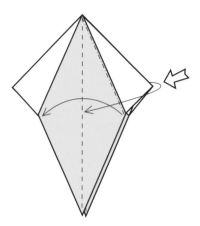

8 Squash the flaps across, valley folding the central crease. Repeat behind.

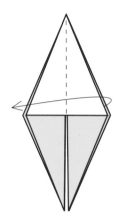

9 Valley fold the flaps across, performing a "minor miracle" fold. (One flap folds to the left on the front and the back.)

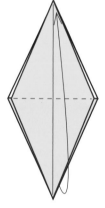

10 Valley fold the bottom corner up to the top. Repeat behind.

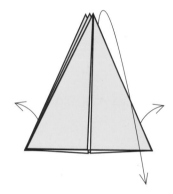

11 Pull out all four sides as far as they will go, making the unit three-dimensional. The model will not lie flat.

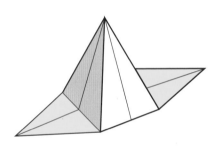

12 The completed module!

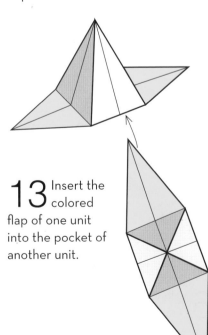

13 Insert the colored flap of one unit into the pocket of another unit.

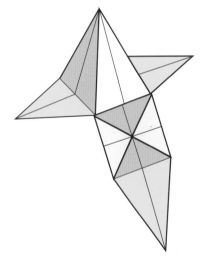

14 Continue this process with the other four units. (There are six units in total.)

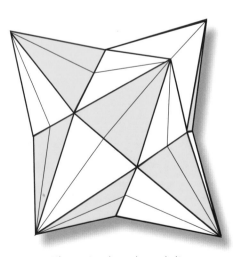

The completed model!

ELEPHANT

This model is the result of several years of work spent trying to develop a simple animal origami. My models usually tend to be geometric, symmetrical, and more complicated, but I realized that I needed to start making some more simple, universal models. This elephant model is based on a preliminary base and, eventually, half of a bird base. It is very fun to do, and, as fun as it is to do, it is just as easy.

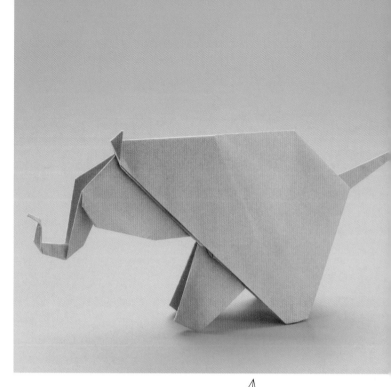

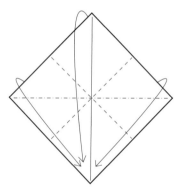

1 Recommended paper: a 6-inch square. Squash the model into a preliminary base.

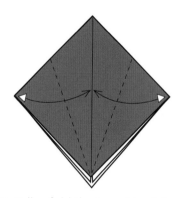

2 Valley fold the two sides into the center. Unfold.

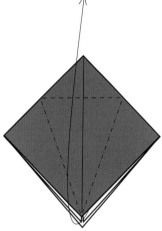

3 Petal fold the top layer, forming half of a bird base.

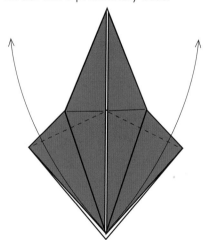

4 Valley fold the two bottom corners of the half-bird base up as far as they can go.

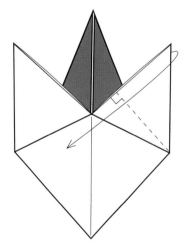

5 Valley fold one of the corners down at a right angle to itself.

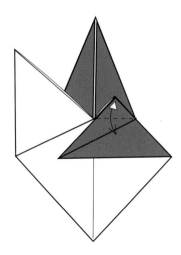

6 Valley fold the corner down. Unfold.

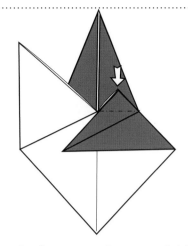

7 Perform an inside reverse fold on the flap you just pre-creased.

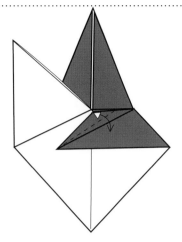

8 Valley fold the raw edge of the flap which will become the leg down slightly past its edge. Unfold.

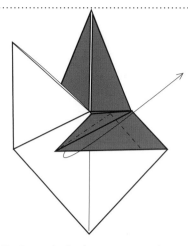

9 Squash the leg up using the crease you made in the previous step.

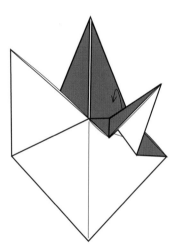

10 Pull out one layer of paper from behind the leg flap.

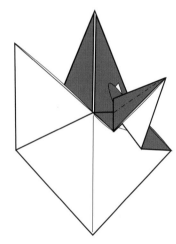

11 Inside reverse fold part of the flap into the pocket.

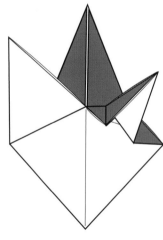

12 Note: this is not the same position you were in at the beginning of step 10. Repeat steps 5–11 on the other side.

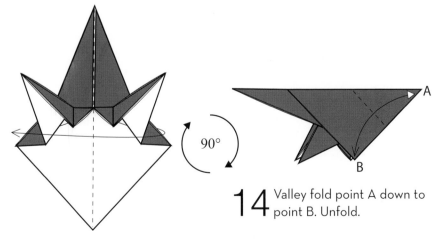

13 Valley fold the model in half.

14 Valley fold point A down to point B. Unfold.

15 Inside reverse fold this flap.

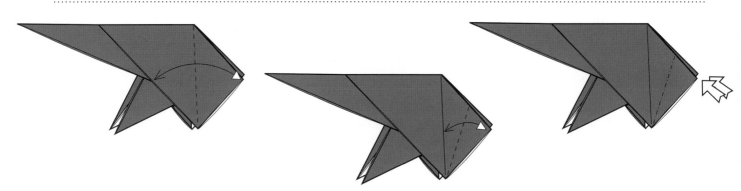

16 Swing the flap over, making a valley fold. Then unfold. Repeat behind.

17 Valley fold the raw edge over to the crease you just made. Then unfold. Repeat behind.

18 Reverse fold the two flaps that will become the hind legs using the creases you made in step 17.

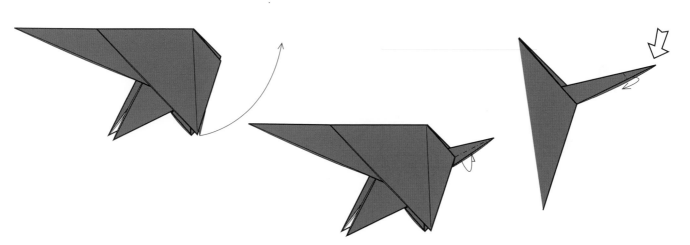

19 Reverse fold the flap that will be the tail. As the landmarks are not visible in this diagram, gauge it yourself.

20 Mountain fold the excess paper inside the tail.

21 Squash the tail flap down, forming the tuft of the tail.

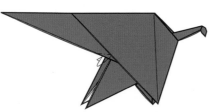

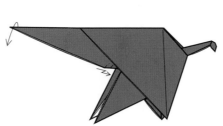

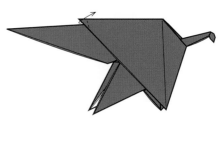

22 Mountain fold some paper on the body as far as it can go, slimming it. Repeat behind.

23 Swing the flap that will be the head down, performing several mountain folds.

24 Reverse fold the tip of the flap.

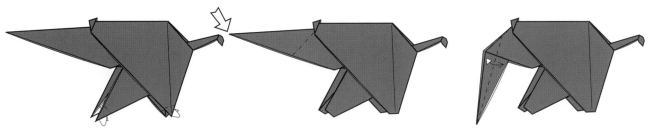

25 Mountain fold the tips of each of the legs.

26 Perform a reverse fold on what will be the head and trunk.

27 Valley fold the top layer of the trunk to the edge. Then unfold. Repeat behind.

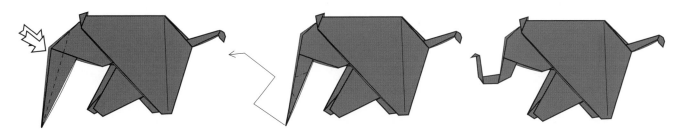

28 Reverse fold the trunk along the crease you made in step 27. Repeat behind.

29 Perform a series of reverse folds, shaping the trunk (for more detail, see the next step).

30 Shape to taste.

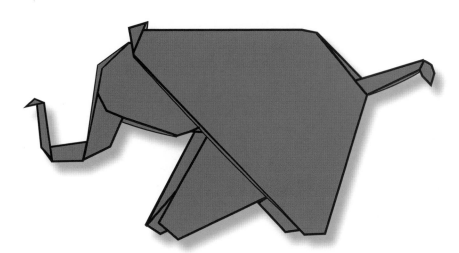

The completed model!

Part II

INTERMEDIATE FOLDS

SITTING DOG

I have always wanted a pet, and just recently my family got a dog: a beagle named Denver. Dogs have always fascinated me, and this is my first pet! I have seen many dog origami models in the past, but none seem to be in the most common position for a dog: sitting down. In designing this model, I think I realized why this was; a sitting dog is an incredibly hard thing to make out of paper! So I tried and tried to create a seated origami dog. It took a long time, but I finally found a base that worked: it's a wonderful base, and if you experiment, you'll find that you can make almost any four-legged animal with it.

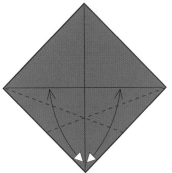

1 Recommended paper: a 6-inch square. Start color side up. Fold the two bottom edges up to the center crease. Unfold.

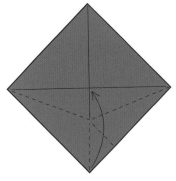

2 Squash the bottom corner in to the center, forming half of a simple fish base.

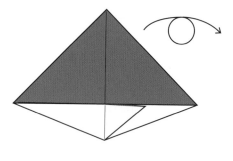

3 Flip the model over.

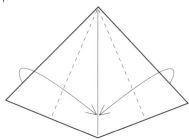

4 Valley fold the left and right sides of the model into the center crease.

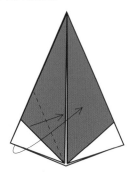

5 Valley fold the bottom left edge of the model up and to the center, aligning where the white meets the colored part of the paper with the center.

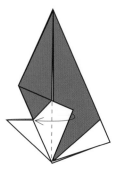

6 Valley fold the flap back over across the center.

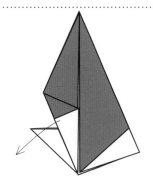 **7** Unfold back to step 5.

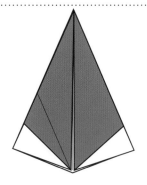 **8** Repeat steps 5–7 on the other side.

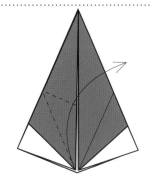 **9** Swing the left flap up and across.

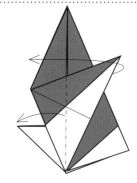 **10** Squash the flap across along its central crease.

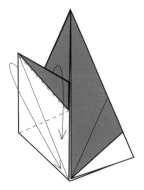 **11** Squash the flap down, using the creases you made in steps 5–8.

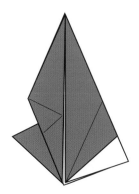 **12** Repeat steps 9–11 on the other side.

13 Flip the model over.

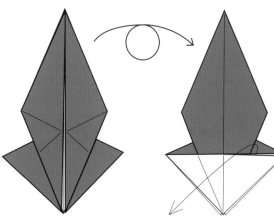 **14** Pull forward the triangular white flap, opening up the bottom of the model.

 **15** Collapse the flap back so that it lies flat.

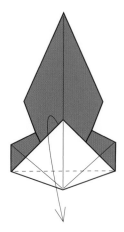 **16** Valley fold the flap down as far as it will go.

17 Flip the model over.

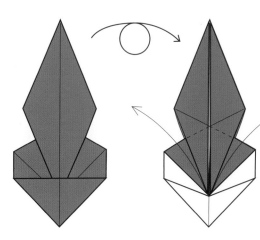 **18** Valley fold the two colored flaps up and out as far as they will go.

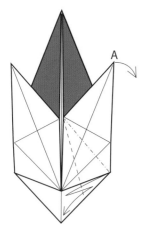

19 Swivel point A to the right and down, making a mountain and valley fold.

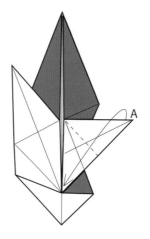

20 Valley fold point A down as far as it will go.

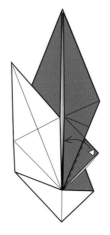

21 Valley fold the flap up along the edge. Unfold.

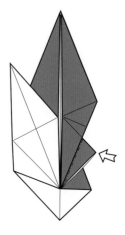

22 Reverse fold the flap inside along the crease you made in step 21.

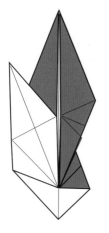

23 Repeat steps 19–22 on the other side.

24 Flip the model over.

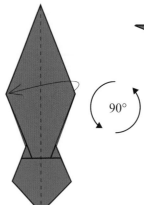

25 Valley fold the model in half.

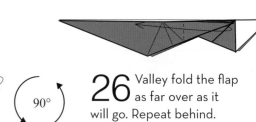

26 Valley fold the flap as far over as it will go. Repeat behind.

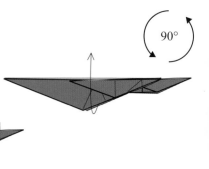

27 Inside reverse fold the end of the model. Repeat behind.

28 Squash the flap up, spreading the layers apart (see next step for details). Repeat behind.

29 Collapse the flap back down. Repeat behind.

30 Open the model up, bringing it to the same position held back in step 25.

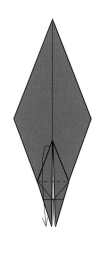

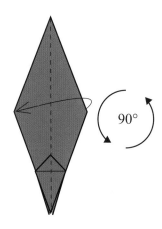

31 Collapse the bottom of the model up, bringing the two sides in to the center.

32 Valley fold the top of the flap you just created down to the bottom.

33 Unsink the center of the small group of layers.

34 Valley fold the model in half.

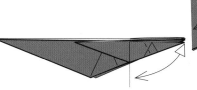

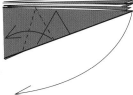

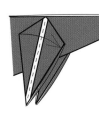

35 Valley fold the left tip of the model down and over so that it rests a little bit before the invisible line that is an extension of the line above. Unfold. Repeat behind.

36 Squash the flap over using the crease you made in step 35. Repeat behind.

37 Valley fold the left side of the leg flap over and into the pocket. Repeat behind.

38 Valley fold the right tip of the central flap down and over along the invisible line that is an extension of the line above. Unfold. Repeat behind.

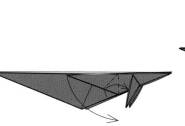

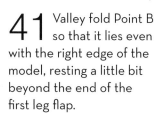

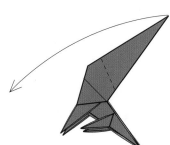

39 Squash the flap over along the crease you made in step 38. Repeat behind.

40 Valley fold the right side of the leg flap over and inside the pocket. Repeat behind.

41 Valley fold Point B so that it lies even with the right edge of the model, resting a little bit beyond the end of the first leg flap.

42 Valley fold the top point over down along its top edge.

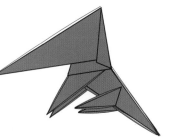

43 Valley fold the right side of the head over, creasing from point C to point D.

44 Unfold back to step 41.

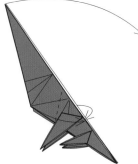

45 Wrap the paper around along the crease you made in step 41.

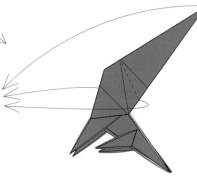

46 Wrap the paper around along the crease you made in step 42.

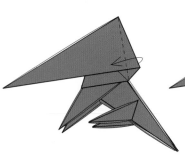

47 Valley fold the right side of the head over along the crease you made in step 43. Repeat behind.

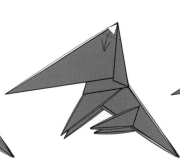

48 Valley fold the top of the head down. Unfold.

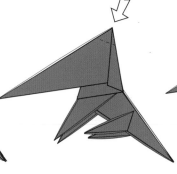
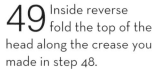

49 Inside reverse fold the top of the head along the crease you made in step 48.

50 Bring the leg out from under the layer of paper near the head. Repeat behind.

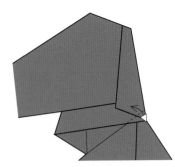

51 Valley fold the bottom tip of the ear up along the underlying crease. Unfold. Repeat behind.

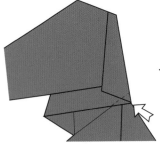

52 Reverse fold the tip of the ear inside along the crease you made in step 51. Repeat behind.

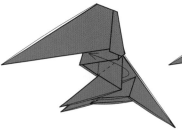

53 Valley fold the leg flap back along its hinge, allowing it to rest within the pocket of the ear made in step 52. Repeat behind.

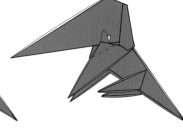

54 Mountain fold the top of the leg, shaping it. Repeat behind.

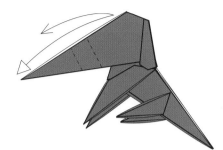

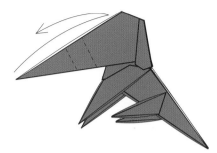

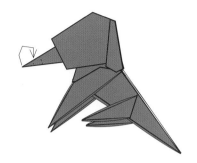

55 Make a mountain fold and then a valley fold, further shaping the head and the snout. Unfold.

56 Make two reverse folds, bringing the left tip of the model inside and then out again.

57 Wrap the paper on the snout around twice, forming the nose.

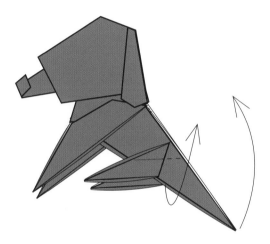

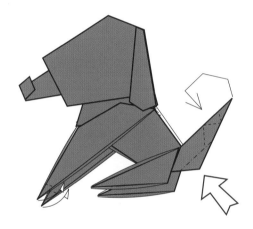

58 Wrap the layers of the tail around, keeping it behind the legs.

59 Shape the model to taste, sinking the tail, making it thinner, curling the tail, rounding off the feet, etc.

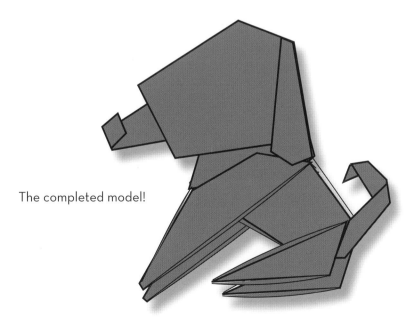

The completed model!

FAMILY OF BIRDS

This model consists of a mother, a father, and a baby (the one in front). I designed it while trying to create a three-headed bird (an endeavor with which I succeeded, but is not shown in this book). I stumbled upon this model serendipitously and liked it so much that I decided to replicate it. I showed it to some people, and they all liked it too (particularly, the baby bird out front).

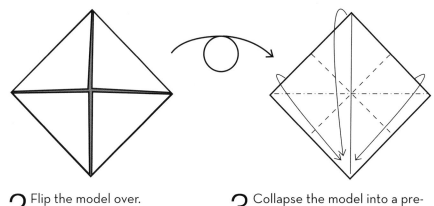

1 Recommended paper: a 6-inch square. Start color side up. Valley fold the four corners of the model into the center, forming a blintz base.

2 Flip the model over.

3 Collapse the model into a preliminary base.

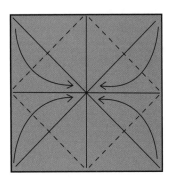

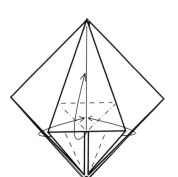

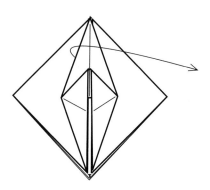

4 Squash one flap over, so that the former edge of the flap lies even with the center.

5 Petal fold the flap up.

6 Unwrap some paper from the central flap, collapsing according to pre-creases.

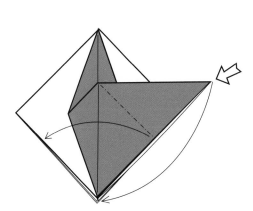

7 Squash the flap down into half of a preliminary base.

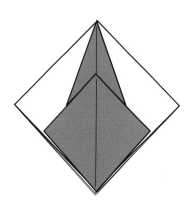

8 Repeat steps 4–7 on the other three large flaps that you created in step 3.

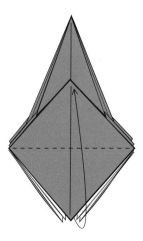

9 Valley fold the central flap up. Repeat behind (but not the other two sides).

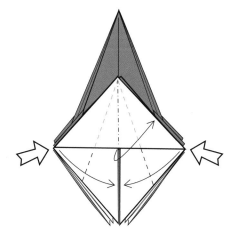

10 Squash the central flap across. Repeat behind.

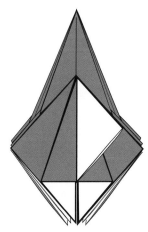

11 Repeat steps 4–6 on this flap, and the identical one behind.

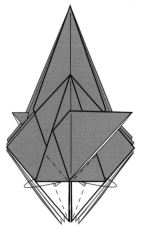

12 Perform two inside reverse folds on the bottom of the central flap. Repeat behind.

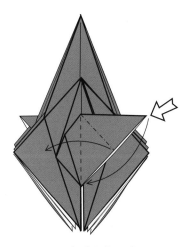

13 Squash the flap down into half of a preliminary base. Repeat behind.

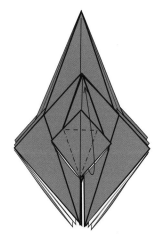

14 Petal fold flap up into half of a bird base. Repeat behind.

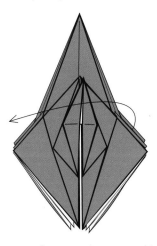

15 Perform a "minor miracle." (Flaps fold to the left on the front and to the right on the back.)

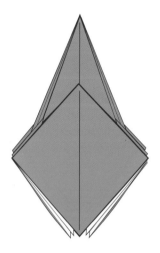

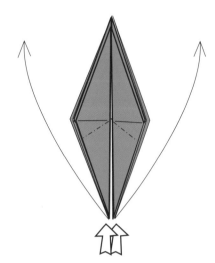

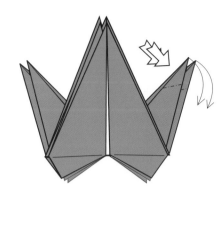

16 Repeat step 14 on the central flap (as well as the one behind).

17 Reverse fold the flaps up on all four flaps.

18 Reverse fold the flap that will be the head. Repeat behind.

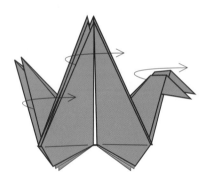

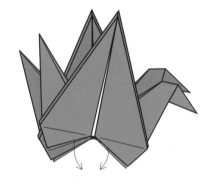

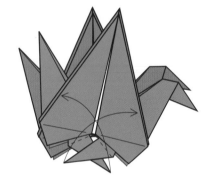

19 Spread the two birds apart, using a series of pivot folds.

20 Bring down the flap that you made in step 14 on each side.

21 Valley fold the two flaps up as far as they will go.

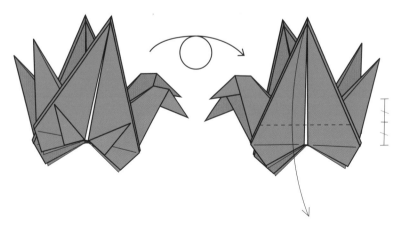

22 Flip the model over.

23 Valley fold the flap down about half of the way.

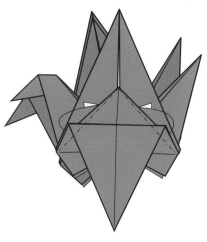

24 Perform two mountain folds, locking the flap into place.

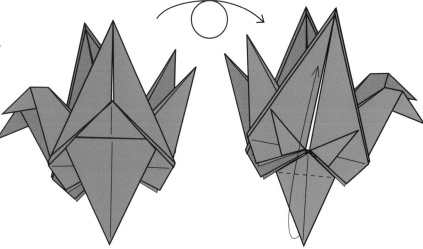

25 Flip the model over.

26 Valley fold the flap up.

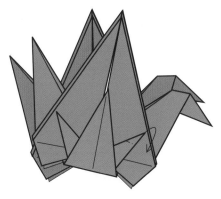

27 Mountain fold the flap that will be the head.

The completed model!

CHECKERBOARD PRISM

This model is based on the fish base, though with some obvious alterations. It is unique and quite vexing to do: partly because it is made up of three-dimensional units, and partly because it has a very complicated connection process. It was named the "checkerboard" prism because it appears, at least to me, like a checkerboard viewed through a prism. Whatever it resembles to you, this is a very enjoyable model to fold.

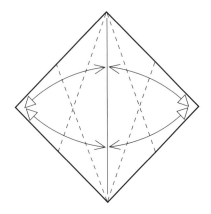

1 Recommended paper: six 6-inch squares. Begin color side down. Fold and unfold each of the sides into the center crease.

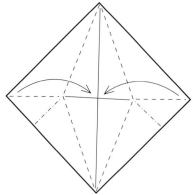

2 Squash each of the opposite corners in to the center, forming a simple fish base.

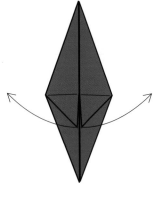

3 Completely unfold the model.

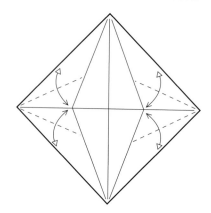

4 Valley fold each side into the center, only creasing to the fish base creases. Unfold.

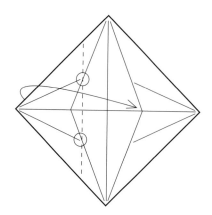

5 Valley fold the left corner in, using the two circled areas, the meeting of the creases from steps 2 and 4, as landmarks.

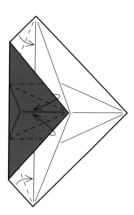

6 Collapse the colored flap, bringing the fish base creases to the center while utilizing the other creases made in step 4.

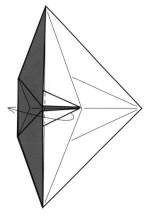

7 Valley fold the flap over.

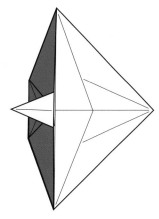

8 Repeat steps 5–7 on the right side.

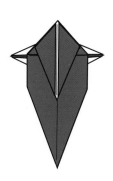

9 Flip the model over.

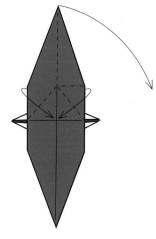

10 Squash the top flap down.

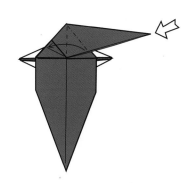

11 Squash the top flap across the center.

12 Unfold back to step 10.

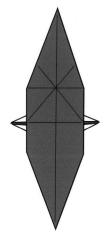

13 Repeat steps 10–12 on the bottom half of the model.

14 Flip the model back over.

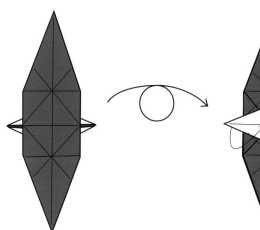

15 Swing the two white flaps up, to the center. The model will not lie flat.

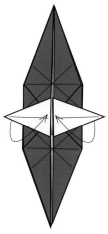

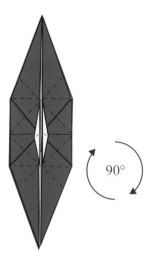

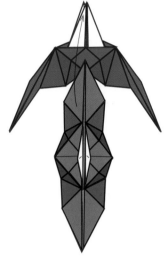

16 Partially collapse the model using the creases that you made in the previous 5 steps.

17 The completed module!

18 Slide the colored triangular flap of one unit into the white triangular pocket of another.

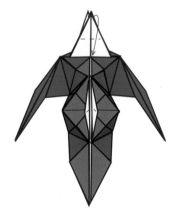

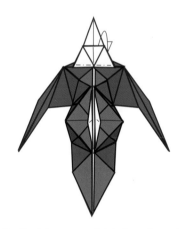

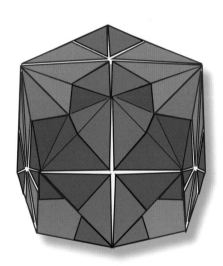

19 Valley fold the white flap down.

20 Mountain fold the white flap behind into the pocket.

The completed model!

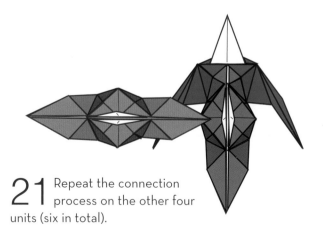

21 Repeat the connection process on the other four units (six in total).

FLAPPING BIRD

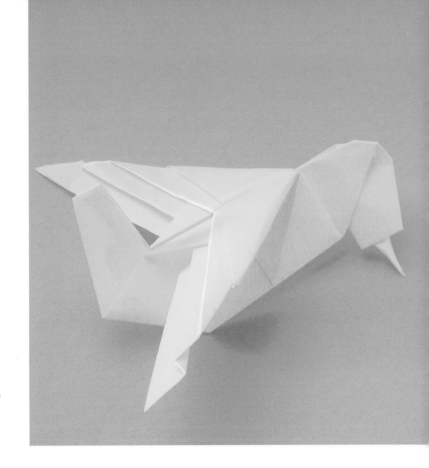

This bird model was created while I was waiting for a piano lesson: I had a piece of paper with me, and I came up with the idea that I should try to fold a bird. However, I knew none by heart (except the simple paper crane), so I was forced to try to create one. The original draft of this model was based on the more conventional bird base, but I could not find a way to swivel the flaps for the wings to be able to move. So I decided to change my original base to the fish base. Lo and behold, by the time I was ready for my piano lesson, I had the following bird model created!

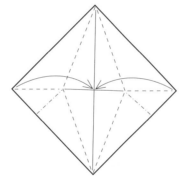

1 Recommended paper: a 6-inch square. Begin color side down. Fold each of the sides into the center crease. Unfold.

2 Squash each of the opposite corners into the center, forming a simple fish base.

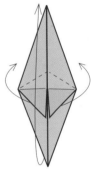

3 Pull the center flaps up so that the central creases become even with the top edges of the model. Try to avoid spreading the bottom half of the model. The model will not lie flat.

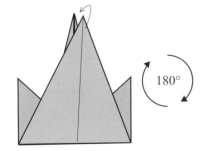

180°

4 Squash the rest of the model so that creases similar to those that appeared in the top half of the model also appear in the bottom half. Do not change the location of the flaps; the model will now lie flat.

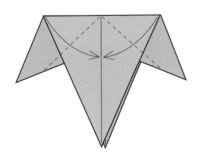

5 Valley the fold the side flaps into the center.

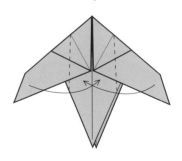

6 Valley fold both of the two side flaps across, while they are still inside their pockets.

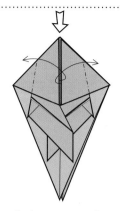

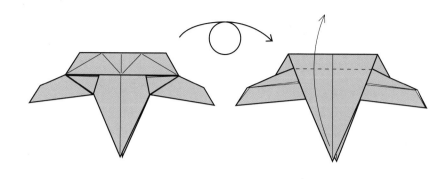

7 Squash the top two flaps outward, valley folding the top down perpendicular to the central crease.

8 Flip the model over.

9 Fold the front flap up as far as it will go.

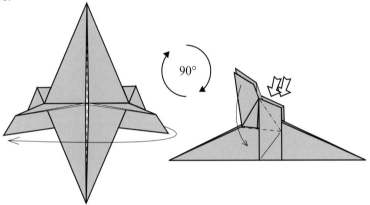

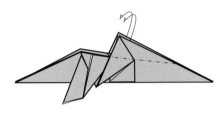

10 Valley fold the model in half.

11 Squash the top flaps down. Repeat behind.

12 Mountain fold the uppermost layer downward. Repeat behind.

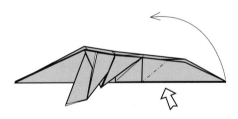

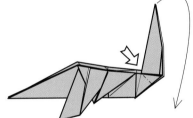

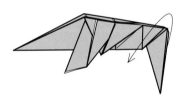

13 Perform an inside reverse fold on the right side of the model. This will later become the head.

14 Perform another inside reverse fold on the soon-to-be head. Gauge your own landmarks for head size.

15 Open up the head.

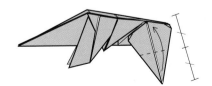

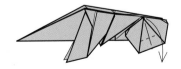

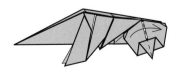

16 Valley fold the head up, at its halfway point.

17 Valley fold what will be the beak back down. Gauge it for the length that you would like for your beak.

18 Valley fold the head back over.

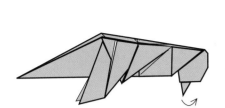

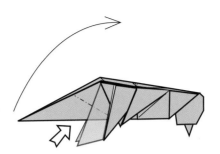

19 Pull the beak across beneath the head, so it lies in the center.

20 Inside reverse fold the flap that will eventually be the tail.

21 Inside reverse fold the flap, shaping the tail.

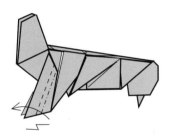

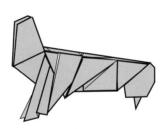

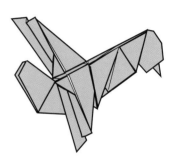

22 Crimp the wings in the general shape of feather ruffles.

23 Shape the bird in any other ways that you desire, making it attractive.

The completed model!

To make the bird flap its wings, grasp where the head meets the body and where the tail meets the body and pull back and forth.

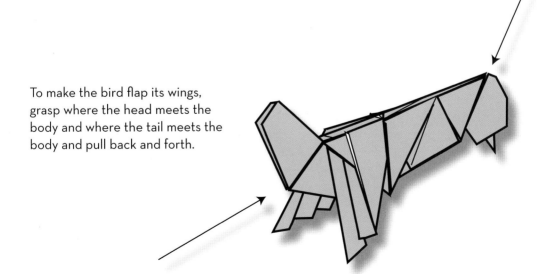

Part III

ADVANCED FOLDS

HEART RING

This model was designed for my mother's birthday, though I had discovered the base several years before. It looks much more difficult than it is, though it requires some precise folding so that it stays together. Be forewarned: if the heart is not correctly formed, is just looks like a blob on top of the ring. A challenge to folders: try to manipulate this model to put a diamond on the top to make it an engagement ring.

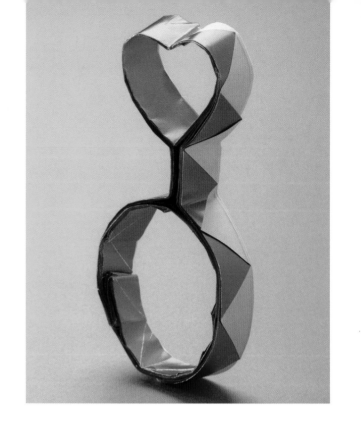

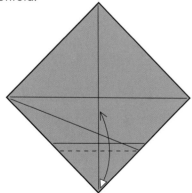

1 Recommended paper: a 10-inch square. Valley fold the bottom corner up to the center. Unfold.

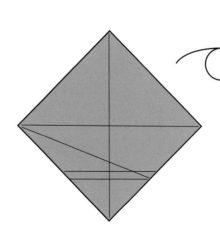

2 Valley fold the bottom right side to the central crease. Unfold.

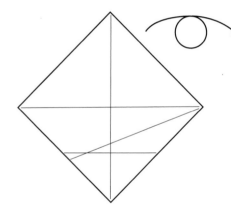

3 Flip the model over.

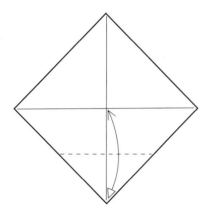

4 Valley fold the bottom corner up along the center edge, using the crease you made in step 2 as a landmark. Unfold.

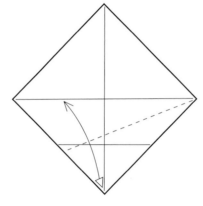

5 Flip the model over.

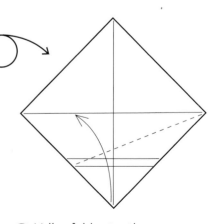

6 Valley fold using the crease you made in step 2.

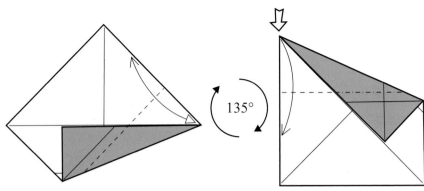

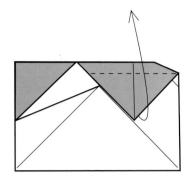

7 Valley fold along the crease you made in step 1. Unfold.

8 Reverse fold the top corner down along the crease you made in step 7.

9 Valley fold up using the crease you made in step 4 as a land-mark.

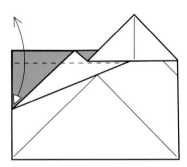

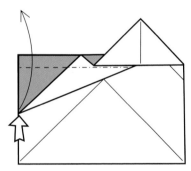

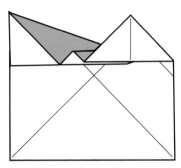

10 Valley fold along the edge formed in step 9. Unfold.

11 Reverse fold the top corner down along the crease you made in step 10.

12 Repeat steps 10–11 on this side, four more times.

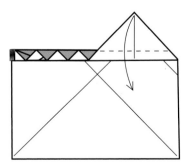

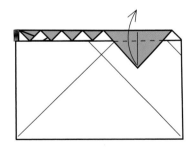

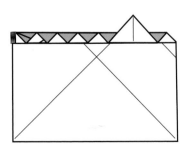

13 Valley fold the triangular flap down using the edge behind it as a landmark.

14 Valley fold the triangular flap up using the edge behind it as a landmark.

15 Repeat steps 13–14 again.

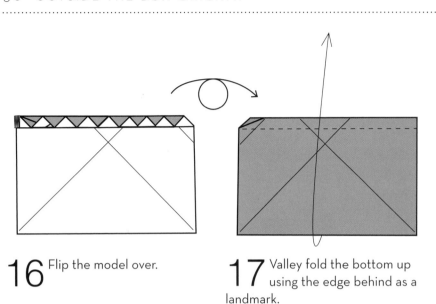

16 Flip the model over.

17 Valley fold the bottom up using the edge behind as a landmark.

18 Valley fold the left side down along the crease you made in step 17. Unfold.

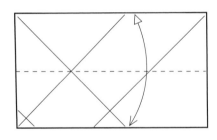

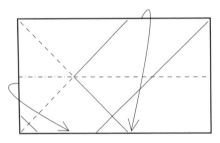

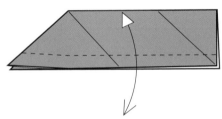

19 Valley fold the top edge down to the bottom. Unfold.

20 Collapse the model down, using the creases you made in the last two steps.

21 Valley fold the model down using the edge behind as a landmark. Unfold.

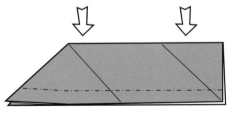

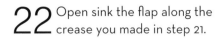

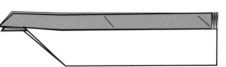

22 Open sink the flap along the crease you made in step 21.

23 Repeat steps 21–22 three more times.

24 Valley fold the right side of the model down to the bottom, creasing through five layers. Unfold.

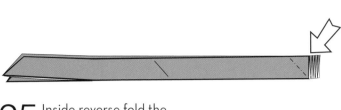

25 Inside reverse fold the top layer along the crease you made in step 24.

26 Repeat step 25 on the other layers.

27 Perform an Elias stretch on the first two flaps. An Elias stretch will create flaps from the pleats by changing their direction 90 degrees.

28 Repeat step 27 three times on the flaps behind.

29 Swing the flaps back to the right.

30 Perform a larger Elias stretch on the first two flaps.

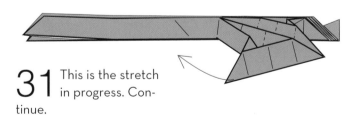

31 This is the stretch in progress. Continue.

32 Repeat step 30, then 29 on each of the layers behind.

33 Perform yet another Elias stretch on each of the layers (don't worry, this one's the last).

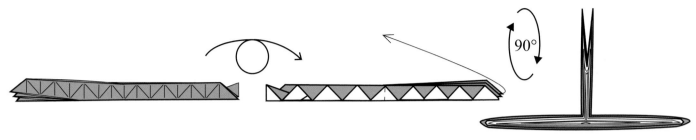

34 (Step 33's process is not shown, but it is the same as was used in previous steps.) Flip the model over.

35 Valley fold the central flap over, across the center. The model should not lie flat.

36 Open the layers on the right side of the model.

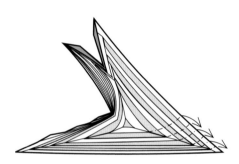

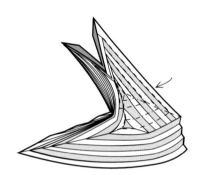

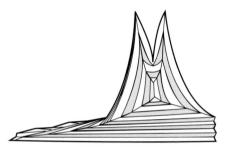

37 Pleat the bottom of the right side of the model (see next step for details).

38 Collapse the model, pleat folding the along the parallel creases (see next step for details).

39 Continue to collapse the model.

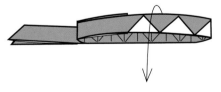

40 Notice the difference between the model at this stage, and the model in step 36. Turn back to the model's position in step 35.

41 Flip the model over.

42 Bring the two top ends of the model together, curving them into a circle.

43 Continue the fold you began in step 42, bringing the right flap into the pocket of the left one.

44 Pivot the band of the ring into the white triangular pocket, making a mountain and valley fold.

45 Bring the side of the ring down, so that the two flaps are pointing up from the ring (see next step for details).

46 Reverse fold the tip of the left flap inside.

47 Bring the tip of the right flap into the pocket of the left flap.

48 Next step shows the model from the top.

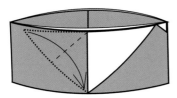

49 Valley fold the inside flap up, locking the two flaps into place.

50 Shape the top loop of the heart into a heart (you might want to add in some creases or even wet fold to make it stay that way).

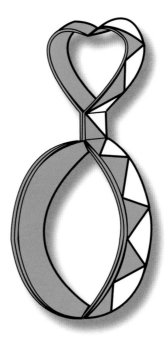

The completed model!

FLORAL DESIGN

This model is the result of an extended effort to make a floral design origami. During this process, I quite accidentally created the snowflake (see page 96). My ideal floral design model had a color change, a general floral shape, and two distinctly different patterns (one on the outside and one on the inside). It took quite a while to create a model that fit each of these requirements, but I eventually succeeded.

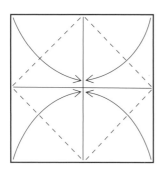

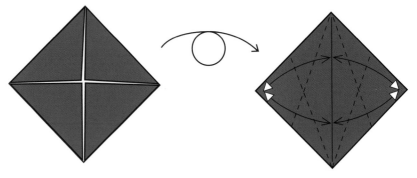

1 Recommended paper: a 10-inch square. Begin color side down. Valley fold the four corners of the model into the center, forming a blintz base.

2 Flip the model over.

3 Fold and unfold each of the sides into the center crease.

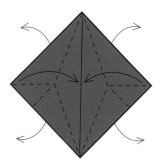

4 Squash each of the opposite corners in to the center, forming a simple fish base, but swinging the four flaps out from underneath.

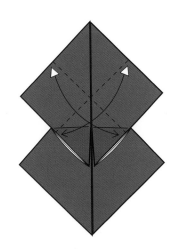

5 Perform two valley folds, folding and unfolding the square in half, both ways.

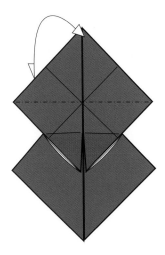

6 Mountain fold the square in half, and then unfold.

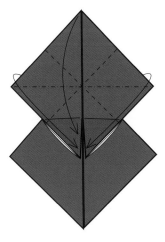

7 Squash the top square into a preliminary base. But only squash the very top layer, and nothing behind.

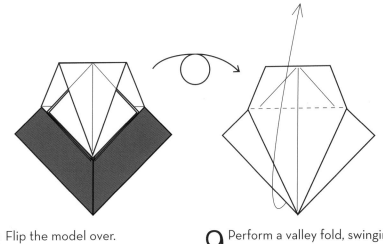

8 Flip the model over.

9 Perform a valley fold, swinging the flap up.

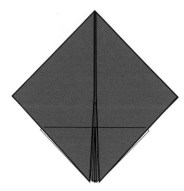

10 Repeat steps 5-7 on this side.

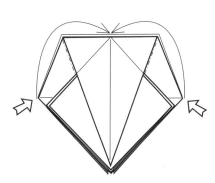

11 Sink the two sides in so that they lie even with the other edges.

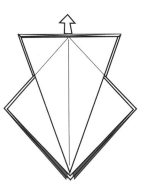

12 Unsink the center of the model.

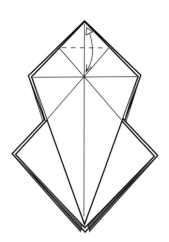

13 Valley fold the top tip down to the specified point. Unfold.

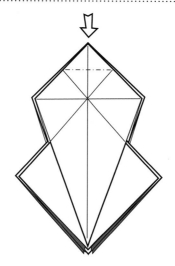

14 Sink the top of the model down along the crease you made in step 13.

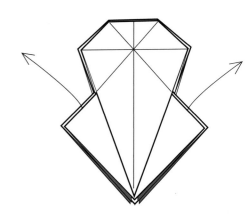

15 Bring the two inner corners of the model out as far as they will go.

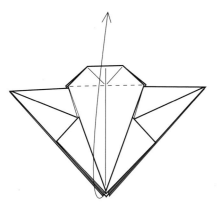

16 Swing the top half of the model up.

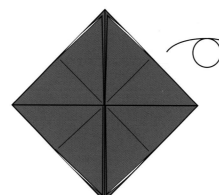

17 Flip the model over.

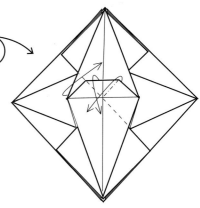

18 Spread the central flaps apart, flattening the center.

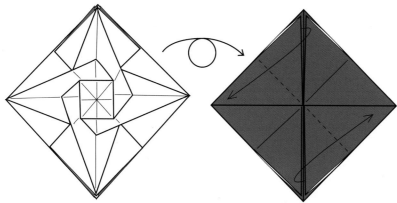

19 Flip the model over.

20 Perform two valley folds, swinging two flaps over.

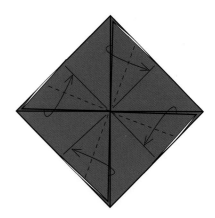

21 Make four valley folds, folding each triangular flap to their respective central crease.

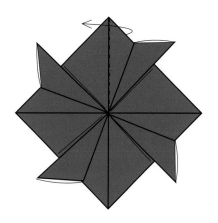

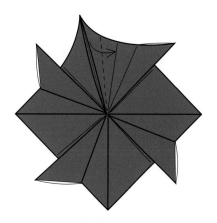

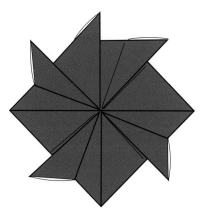

22 Pull out two layers from the top flap.

23 Squash the flap down, valley folding it to the crease.

24 Repeat steps 22–23 on the other three sides.

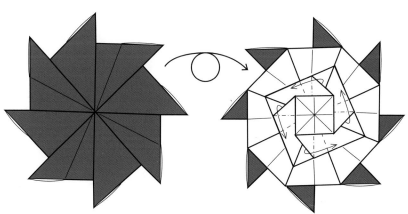

25 Flip the model over.

26 Swing each flap to the left, squashing it down once it has swung as far as it can go.

27 Pull out one layer of paper from one of the triangular flaps, and then squash it back down.

28 Valley fold the flap you just made, under the center of the model.

29 Inside reverse fold the flap (do not sink).

30 Repeat steps 27–29 on the other three sides.

31 Petal fold down this flap, tucking part of it behind one layer.

32 Valley fold the white flap over, but only one layer, pulling it over from inside.

33 Closed sink the top, central white flap across.

34 Closed sink the second, central white flap.

35 Repeat steps 31–34 on the other three similar sides.

36 Repeat steps 31–32 (but not steps 33–34) on all four sides.

37 Valley fold all of the four inner edges of the central octagon, forming a lock.

38 Flip the model over.

39 Valley fold two flaps over on each of the four similar sides alluded to in step 35.

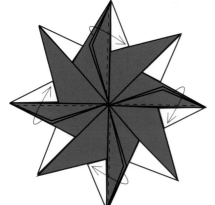

40 Valley fold the two flaps into their respective pockets.

The completed model!

The completed model (on the other side).

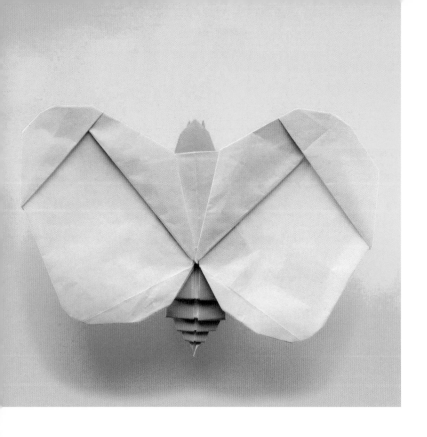

INSECT

I created this insect model several years ago, as a variation of a flower model that I had created. It bears the general name "insect" because I can't decide exactly which type of moth or butterfly it is. The insect is derived from the waterbomb base, with two adjacent flaps being the wings, and the other flaps being the body. It is not too complicated a model, except for the method of creating the wings, which remain three-dimensional for quite a while during the folding process.

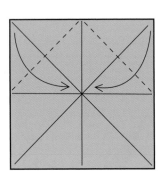

1 Recommended paper: a 10-inch square. Start color side up. Valley fold the top two corners of the model into the center.

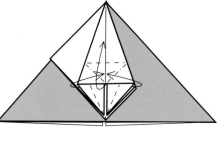

2 Flip the model over.

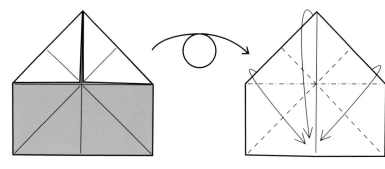

3 Squash the model into half of a waterbomb base.

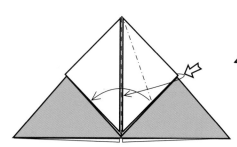

4 Squash one flap over, so that what was formerly the edge of the flap lies even with the center.

5 Petal fold the flap up.

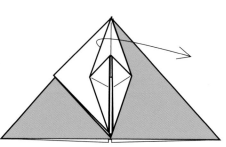

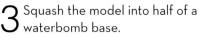

6 Unwrap some paper from the central flap, collapsing according to pre-creases.

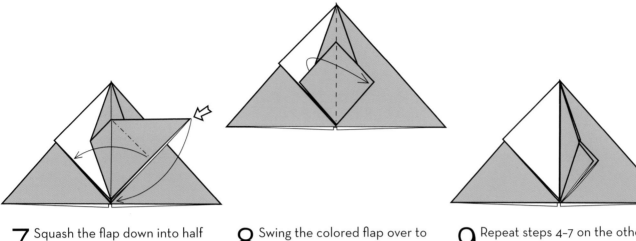

7 Squash the flap down into half of a preliminary base.

8 Swing the colored flap over to the left.

9 Repeat steps 4–7 on the other side.

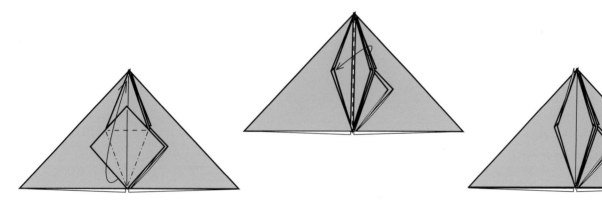

10 Squash the flap up into half of a bird base.

11 Swing two flaps over to the left.

12 Repeat steps 10–11 on the other side.

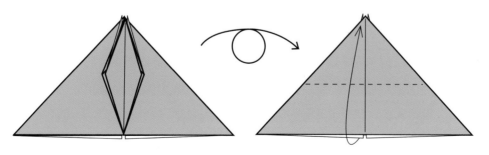

13 Flip the model over.

14 Valley fold the base of the model up almost to the top.

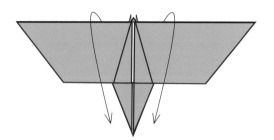

15 Swing one layer of paper down. The model will not lie flat.

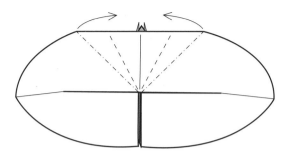

16 Pivot fold the two wings almost to the center.

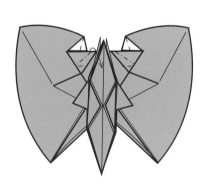

17 Flip the model over.

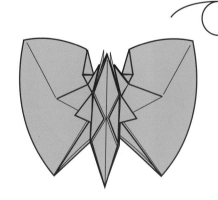

18 Squash the bottom of the wings up, making it flat.

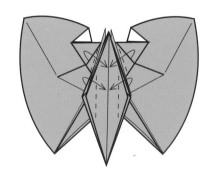

19 Valley fold two flaps to the center on each side. Then pull some paper out around the body and valley fold it to the center.

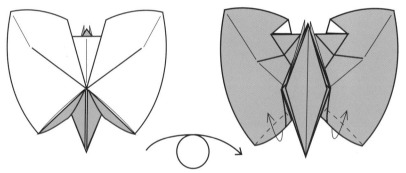

20 Petal fold the flap down, toward you.

21 Flip the model over.

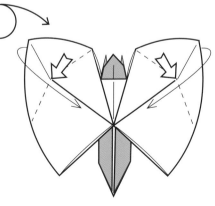

22 Valley fold the wings, squashing them down. The model will (finally) lie flat.

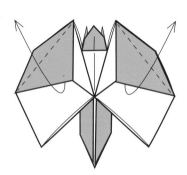

23 Valley fold the wings up.

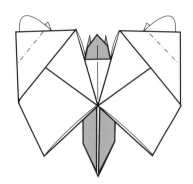

24 Mountain fold the tops of the wings down.

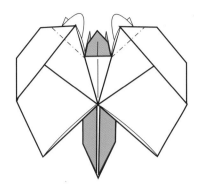

25 Continue to mountain fold the tops of the wings down.

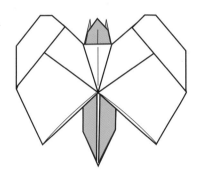

26 Further shape the wings with mountain folds.

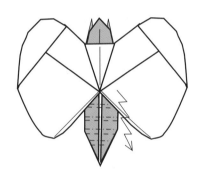

27 Crimp fold the tail.

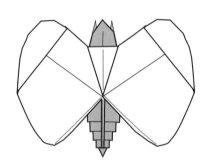

28 Pinch the stinger, shaping it.

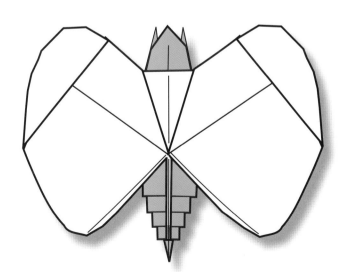

The completed model!

CRANE WITH A CRANE AS A HEAD

I spent a long time trying to figure out a crane model with a crane as a head. This was apparently a lot harder than I thought it would be. I knew I had to use a method similar to the one that I ultimately used, but I just couldn't figure out exactly how I would do it. This model is much simpler in theory than it is when folding, but that supposedly "simple" theory eluded me for several years. But finally—and quite by accident—I figured out how to do this model.

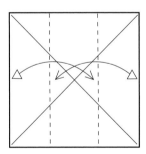

1 Recommended paper: a 10-inch square. Valley fold the two sides in at the ⅓ marks. Unfold.

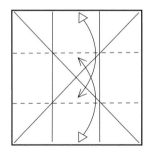

2 Repeat step 1 horizontally.

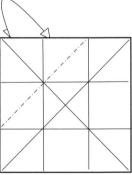

3 Mountain fold the corner behind. Unfold.

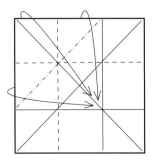

4 Collapse the model along the creases you made in the previous steps.

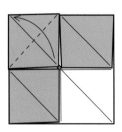

5 Valley fold the central point up as far as it will go.

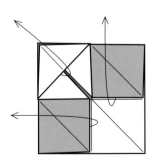

6 Undo the folds you made in step 4.

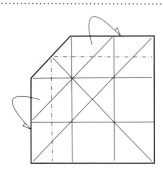

7 Mountain fold the two sides adjacent to the corner down to the ¹/₃ marks.

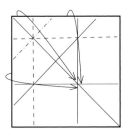

8 Collapse the model along the same lines you did in step 4.

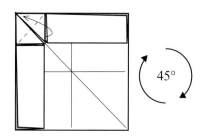

9 Repeat step 5 on this corner.

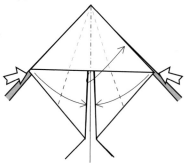

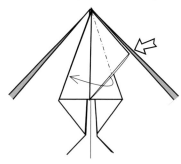

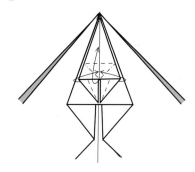

10 Squash the central flap across.

11 Squash one flap over, so that what was formerly the edge of the flap lies even with the central crease.

12 Petal fold the flap up.

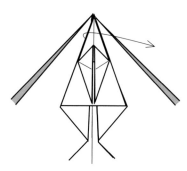

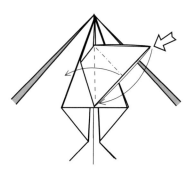

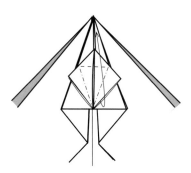

13 Unwrap some paper from around the central flap, collapsing according to pre-creases.

14 Squash the flap down into half of a preliminary base.

15 Petal fold the flap up into half of a bird base.

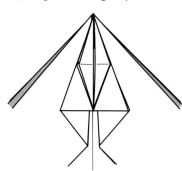

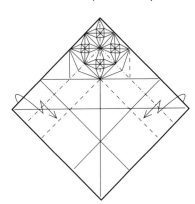

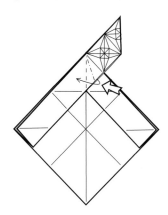

16 Unfold completely (yes, I'm serious).

17 Collapse the model using some creases you made in past steps.

18 Squash the center across.

19 Valley fold the left triangular flap across.

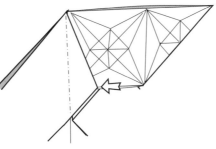

20 Sink the flap you just folded across.

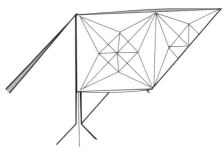

21 Repeat steps 19–20 on the other side.

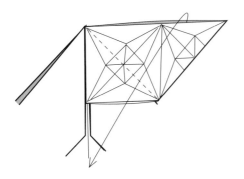

22 Wrap one layer around at the specified crease.

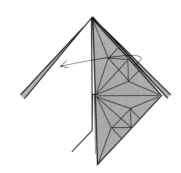

23 Open up the center.

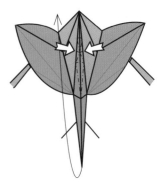

24 Sink the center using the creases as guidelines (see next step for clarification).

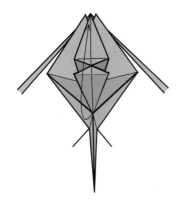

25 Swing the bottom colored part up, flattening the model and completing the sink you started in the last step.

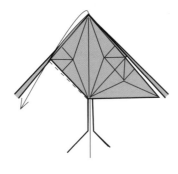

26 Pull out the flap, then collapse it down.

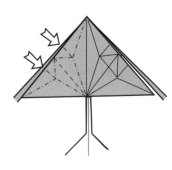

27 Sink the left flap in a similar fashion to the way that you did in step 24 (see next step for details).

28 Swing the left flap up, flattening it out just like you did in step 25.

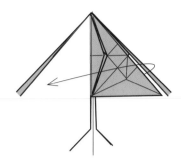

29 Swing the large triangular flap to the left (in doing so, you will also swing over the flap you have just been working on).

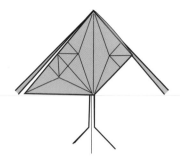

30 Repeat steps 26–29 on this side.

31 Reverse the triangular flap, wrapping it around and up.

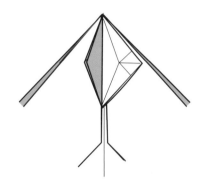

32 Repeat steps 11–15 on the central flap.

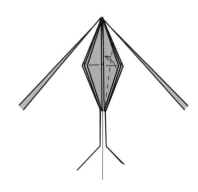

33 Valley fold the right flap to the center.

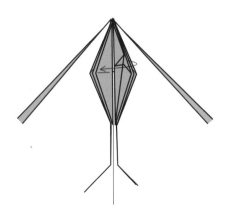

34 Swing two flaps over to the left.

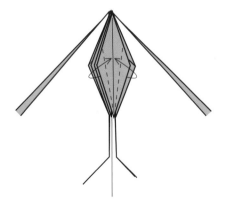

35 Valley fold the two sides into the center.

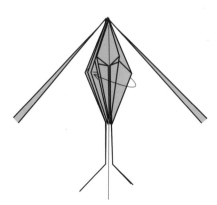

36 Swing two layers over to the left.

37 Valley fold the flap to the edge.

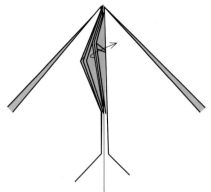

38 Swing four flaps over to the right.

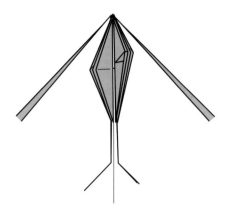

39 Repeat steps 33–38 on the left side.

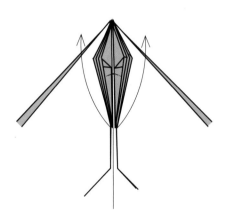

40 Reverse fold each lower flap up as far as they can go.

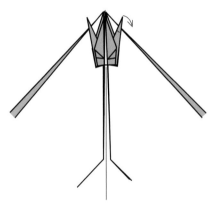

41 Do a small reverse fold to one of the flaps, forming the head.

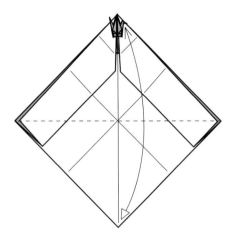

42 Valley fold the whole model up in half. Unfold.

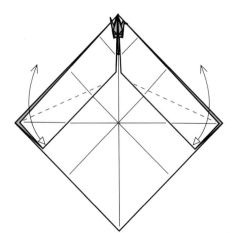

43 Valley fold each flap up (lining up the valley fold with the side). Unfold.

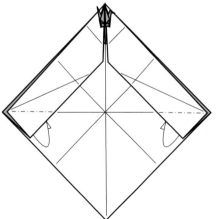

44 Mountain fold each flap under using the specified creases.

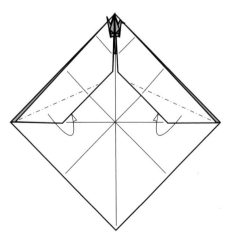

45 Mountain fold each flap under, again, using the other creases.

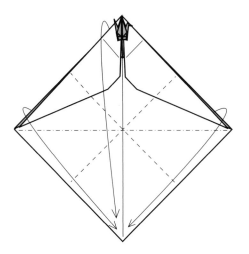

46 Collapse the model into a preliminary base.

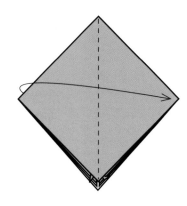

47 Perform a "minor miracle" fold.

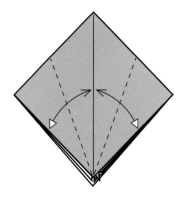

48 Valley fold the two raw edges into the center. Unfold. Repeat behind.

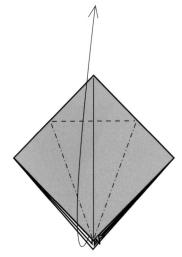

49 Squash the flap up, using the creases you just made as guidelines. Repeat behind. Form a bird base.

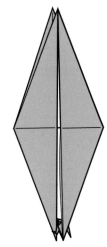

50 Repeat step 35, and then step 40, respectively, on both this side and behind.

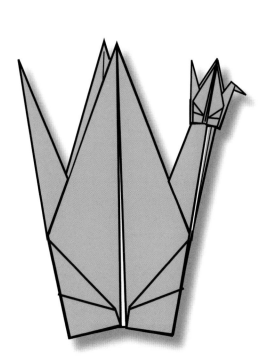

The completed model!

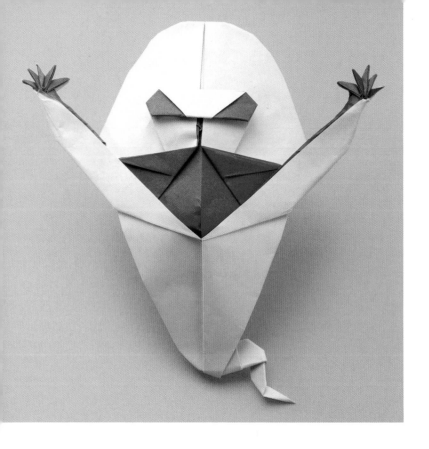

GHOST

This ghost model was based on a relatively simple base, which I have named the "ghost base." It is much like the fish base, but instead of two pairs of congruent flaps, there is only one pair of congruent flaps, and one pair of drastically different sized flaps. It was very fun to design and is equally fun to fold.

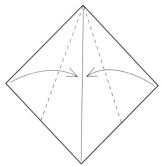  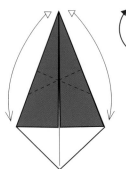 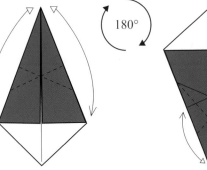 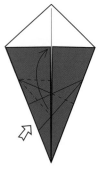

1 Recommended paper: a 10-inch square. Valley fold two of the adjacent sides into the center, forming a kite base.

2 Valley fold the top corner of the model down to each opposite corner. Unfold.

3 Valley fold the edges along the creases you just made. Unfold.

4 Squash the bottom point of the model while spreading apart the central flaps.

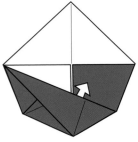 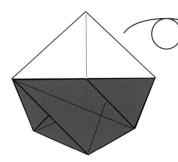 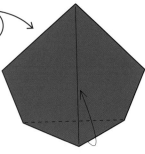

5 Squash the top flap back over.

6 Pull out some trapped paper, so that both sides are symmetrical.

7 Flip the model over.

8 Valley fold the bottom up, using the nearest corners as landmarks. Pull out the flaps from behind, while doing so.

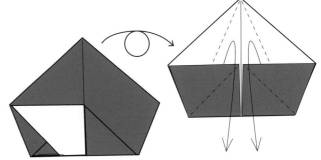

9 Fold the bottom part of the model up (using the same landmarks as the last step).

10 Pull the triangular flap through and collapse it back down.

11 Flip the model over.

12 Perform two partial "rabbit-ears."

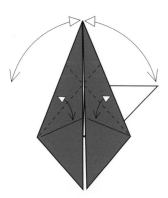

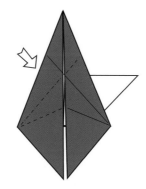

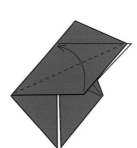

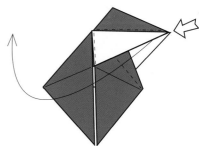

13 Valley fold the top point down using the central creases as guidelines (fold almost to them). Unfold.

14 Squash one of the sides down, as shown above.

15 Valley fold the flap back up.

16 Squash the top flap back over.

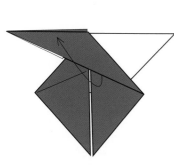

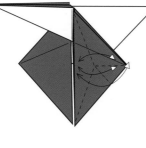

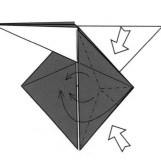

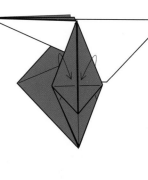

17 Pull out some loose paper under the top flap and collapse it back down.

18 "Rabbit-ear" the right flap. Unfold.

19 Squash the flap using the creases you made in the last step. Spread the internal layers so that when the model lies flat, the internal layers lie symmetrically.

20 Wrap the paper around the flap you just made.

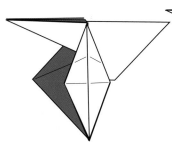

21 Repeat steps 18–20 on the other side.

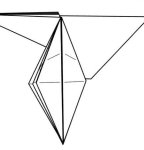

22 Spread the entire model, undoing all of the most primary squash folds.

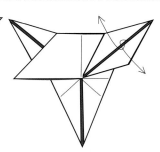

23 Spread the layers of the upper-right part of the model.

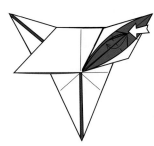

24 Squash some internal flaps inside the upper-right part as shown.

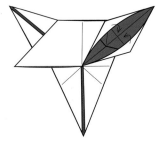

25 Re-collapse the upper-right part.

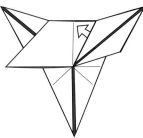

26 Unsink an internal flap within the upper-right part of the model.

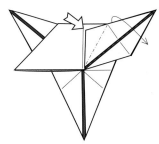

27 Squash the upper-right flap back over.

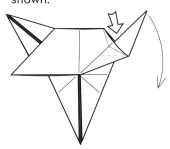

28 Perform an inside-reverse fold on the upper-right flap of the model.

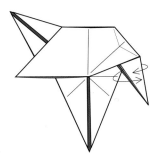

29 Release some paper trapped in the right flap.

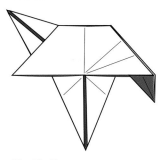

30 Repeat steps 23–29 on the other side.

31 Unlock some trapped paper in the upper-right corner.

32 Squash that corner back down.

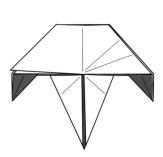

33 Repeat steps 31–32 on the other side.

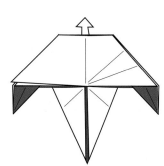

34 Unsink the top layers, and collapse them symmetrically.

35 Wrap one layer of paper around, as shown, on the central flap.

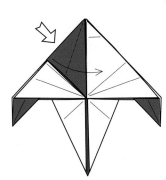

36 Squash the central flap.

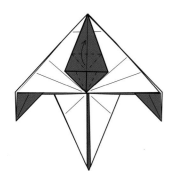

37 Petal fold the central flap.

38 Wrap some paper around the central flap.

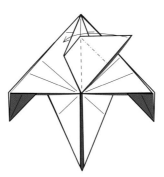

39 Form the paper into half of a preliminary base.

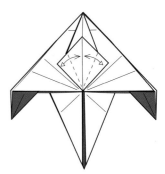

40 Valley fold the sides into the center. Unfold.

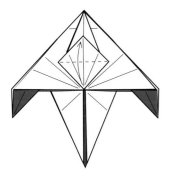

41 Valley fold the paper up.

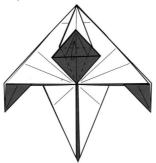

42 Perform a partial petal fold.

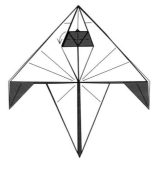

43 Valley fold the flap down.

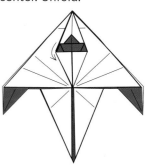

44 Swing the central flap down.

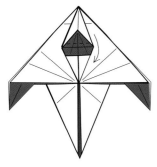

45 Valley fold one layer.

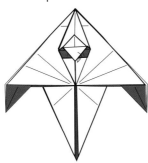

46 Mountain fold the tip uderneath.

47 Open sink the triangular flap near the eyes.

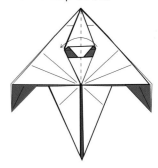

48 Fold two central flaps over.

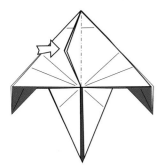

49 Closed sink the right flap. Then, swing the other flap back to the center, maintaining symmetry.

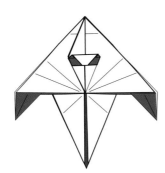

50 Repeat steps 48–49 on the other side.

51 Valley fold the two corners of what will be the mouth up to a landmark that will determine the shape and size of the mouth.

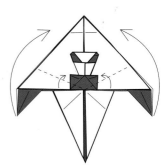

52 Fold what will be the arms up, so that the base of the arms touch the corners of the flaps that you made in step 51.

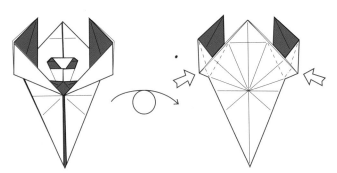

53 Flip the model over.

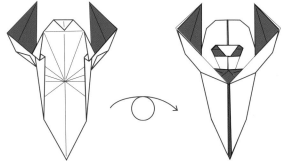

54 Perform a squash fold. Repeat on the other side.

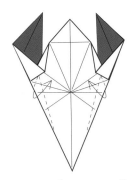

55 Perform a small inside reverse fold under each arm, shaping the body.

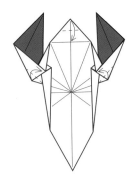

56 Shape the model accordingly, using various valley folds.

57 Flip the model over.

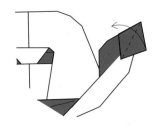

58 Further shape the head, using mountain folds.

59 Valley fold the flap across at the $3/4$ point, and then valley fold back at what was formerly the halfway point. Unfold.

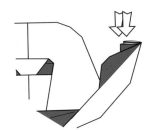

60 Sink in and out, and let the model lie flat.

61 Precrease twice. Repeat behind.

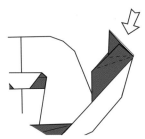

62 Sink in and out. Repeat behind.

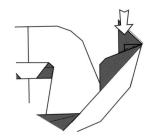

63 Sink in the tiny flap. Repeat behind.

64 Open the small, central flap of the hand.

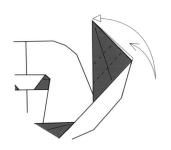

65 Squash the flap down as far as it will go.

66 Valley fold the hand flap up.

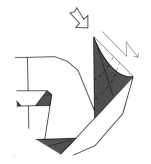

67 Squash the flap over.

68 Make two small inside-reverse folds.

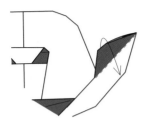

69 Valley fold the hand over.

70 Spread the fingers apart.

71 Wrap some paper around the arm.

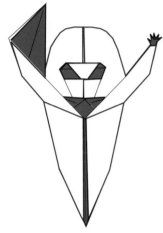

72 Repeat steps 59-71 on the other hand.

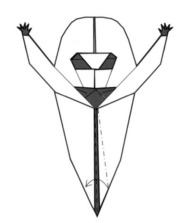

73 Bring one of the sides of the model over the other. The model will not lie flat.

74 Shape the bottom of the model in a shape characteristic of a wisp of smoke.

The completed model—boo!

Part IV

·················

EXPERT FOLDS

FLOWER WITH STEM AND GRASS

I designed this model while sitting on the couch during a vacation in New York. I saw a commercial that (for some odd reason) featured a Monet landscape painting with several distinct flowers poking out of the thick, lustrous grass. I had been just doodling around with a piece of origami paper and thought "Hey, why not? I could make a flower model!" So, a couple hours of television and several pieces of paper later, I had my flower model. It is exceptionally simple in theory, with half of the model devoted to the grass, and the other half devoted to the flower and stem. This flower model works best with one side pink and one side green (as shown in these diagrams).

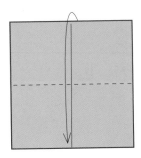

1 Recommended paper: a 10-inch square. Valley fold the model in half.

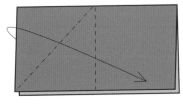

2 Squash the top layer across, forming half of a waterbomb base.

3 Petal fold the bottom up.

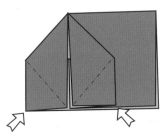

4 Reverse fold both sides of the top layer.

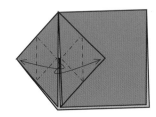

5 Petal fold each side of the top layer simultaneously.

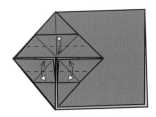

6 Valley fold each side of the top layers to the center. Unfold.

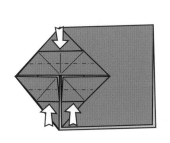

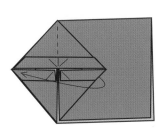

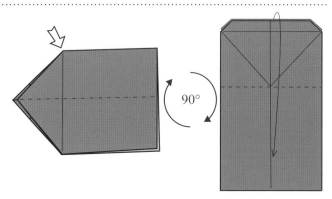

7 Open sink the three sections that you just creased.

8 Swing the flap over to the left, valley folding it.

9 Collapse the model, sinking the top and spreading the two bottom layers to the center.

10 Valley fold the top down.

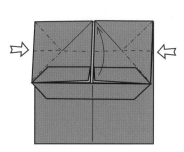

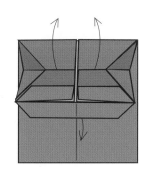

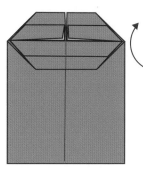

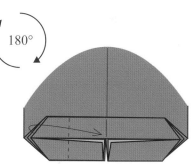

11 Sink both sides of the top layer in, sinking it in half.

12 Continue step 11 (as shown in progress), bringing down the bottom half of the flap (see next step for details).

13 Repeat steps 6-7 on the second set of flaps.

14 Valley fold the top left flap over as far as it will go.

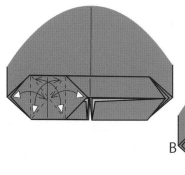

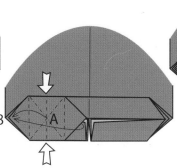

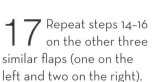

15 Make four valley folds. Unfold.

16 Swing the flap back over. In doing so, bring the central point A to lie even with point B.

17 Repeat steps 14-16 on the other three similar flaps (one on the left and two on the right).

18 Valley fold each side of the top layer to the center. Unfold.

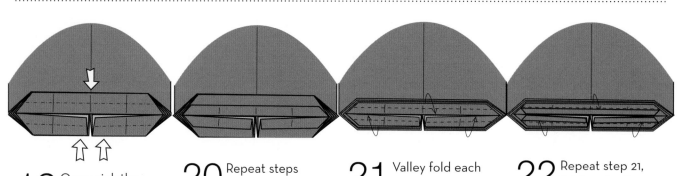

19 Open sink the three sections that you just creased.

20 Repeat steps 18–19 on the three layers behind, and then repeat steps 14–16 on every side.

21 Valley fold each side of the top layer down to the center.

22 Repeat step 21, folding the flaps behind the other ones.

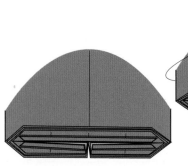

23 Repeat step 21 on the other six layers that are behind.

24 Turn the model to see the side view.

25 (Only the bottom half is shown.) Stretch the model down, valley folding down the middle, but also forming a square of valley folds in the center of each section.

26 (Only the bottom half is shown.) Swing the model back to a front view.

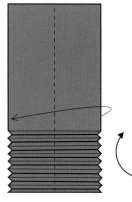

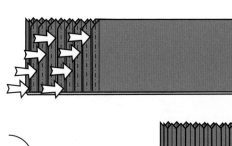

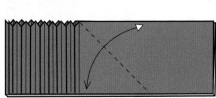

27 Closed sink the eight flaps of what will become the grass.

28 Valley fold the model in half.

90°

29 Repeat step 27 on this side and behind.

30 Valley fold the top edge down to lie even with the right-most crease of the clump of grass. Unfold.

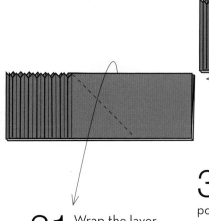

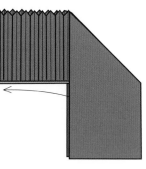

32 Pull out one layer of paper from the pocket. Repeat behind.

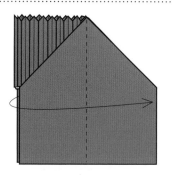

33 Valley fold the flap over to the right. Repeat behind.

34 Valley fold all three layers to the left, dividing the section into eighths. Unfold. Repeat behind.

31 Wrap the layer around using the crease you made in step 30.

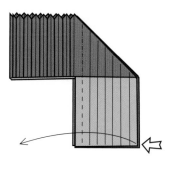

35 Perform a reverse fold on the top layer, bringing it across. Repeat behind.

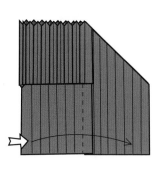

36 Repeat step 35 on the flap, bringing it back across. Repeat behind, and then repeat steps 35–36, sinking and unsinking the middle flap.

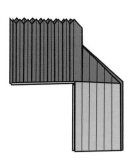

37 Repeat steps 35–36 on the flap two more times, and then 35 one last time, repeating behind and on the center flap. (This is not for the faint of heart).

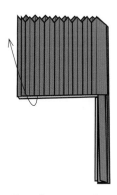

38 Lift up one flap, spreading apart the layers that you just creased.

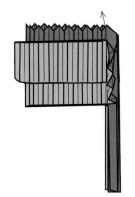

39 Stretch the flap up as far as it will go, performing an Elias stretch.

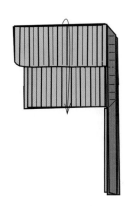

40 Valley fold the flap back down.

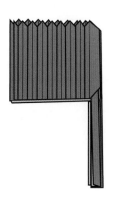

41 Repeat steps 38–40 on the other side.

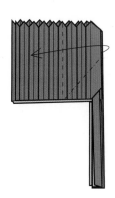

42 Squash the right half of the model over as far as it will go.

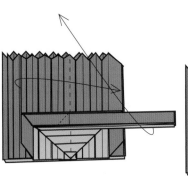

43 Squash the flap up while swinging the layer back across.

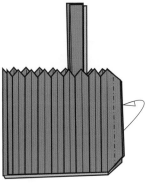

44 Mountain fold the flap behind. Repeat behind.

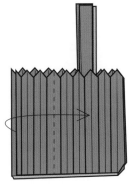

45 Squash the top layer over.

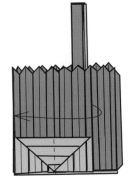

46 Valley fold the model back across.

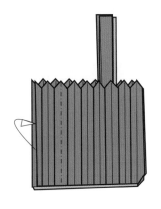

47 Mountain fold the flap behind. Repeat behind.

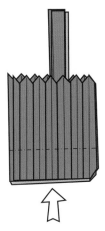

48 Inside reverse fold the lower part of the top layer as far in as it will go. Repeat behind.

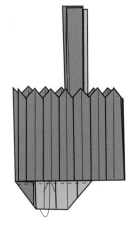

49 Valley fold the remaining lower flap under and into the pocket.

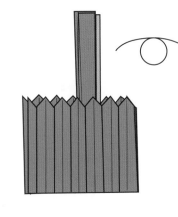

50 Flip the model over.

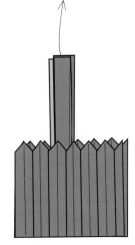

51 Pull the flap that will be the stem up as far as it will go.

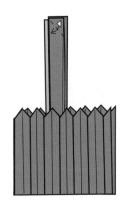

52 Valley fold the top five corners down so that their tops lie even with the left side. Unfold.

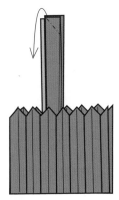

53 Open up the top five layers, using the creases you made in the last step. The model will not lie flat.

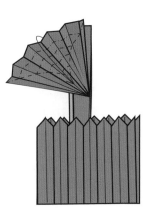

54 Stretch the edges, pulling them down as far as they will go, using the crease you made in step 52 as a guide.

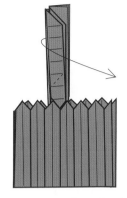

55 Valley fold the flap over at its hinge.

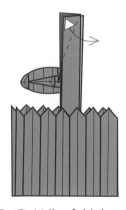

56 Flip the model over.

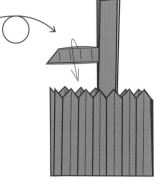
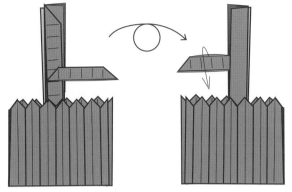

57 Bring the top layer of the flap that will be the leaf over and down. The leaf will not lie flat.

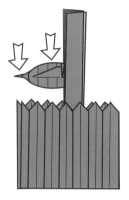

58 Make two squash folds, so that the leaf will now lie flat.

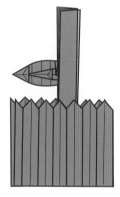

59 Round off the leaf, giving it an organic quality.

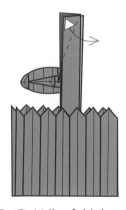

60 Valley fold the remaining eleven flaps down from the top right corner to a point slightly above the top of the leaf. Unfold.

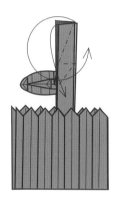

61 Spread all eleven layers of the top of the stem apart, using the crease you made in step 60 as a landmark for squashing it down.

62 Tuck the excess flap (or flaps, depending upon how precisely your creases were) into the nearest respective pocket.

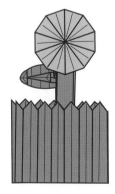

63 Continue to shape the model, squashing the head of the flower, the stem, the grass, and pulling down the leaf.

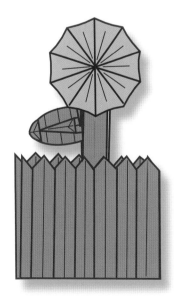

The completed model!

WEAVE DESIGN

I designed this piece while sitting on my grand-parents' couch in New Jersey. I was watching television and just doing random folds when I stumbled across this model. The weave design is an intellectually stimulating model because it looks like it would be impossible to create from a single piece of paper—or a square piece of paper, at that. Nevertheless, here the model is... enjoy!

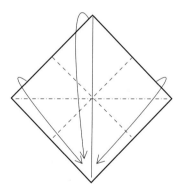

1 Recommended paper: a 10-inch square. Squash the model into a preliminary base.

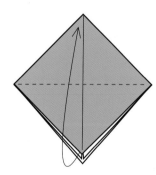

2 Valley fold the flap up. Repeat behind.

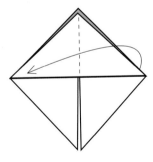

3 Swing one flap over to the left. Repeat behind, performing a "minor miracle."

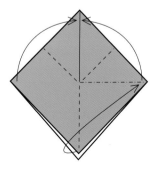

4 Squash the flap up. Repeat behind.

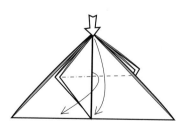

5 Squash the central flap down. Repeat behind.

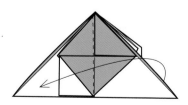

6 Repeat step 3 on the central flap (as well as the one behind).

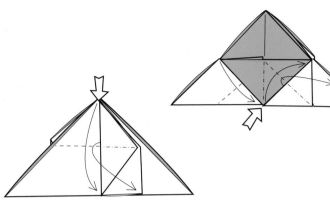

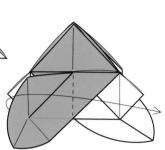

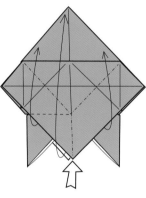

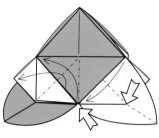

7 Repeat step 5 on the central flap (as well as the one behind).

8 Squash the central flap up and away. Repeat behind. The model will not lie flat.

9 Swing the three-dimensional flap to the right. Repeat behind.

10 Repeat step 8 on this side of the central flap, completing the complex squash fold you started in step 8. Repeat behind.

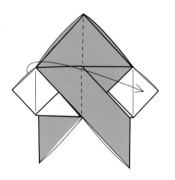

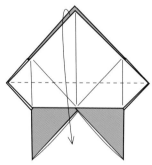

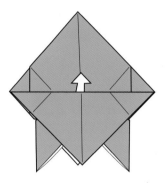

11 Swing one flap to the right. Repeat behind.

12 Valley fold the central flap down. Repeat behind.

13 Sink (or rather, unsink) the flap out of the center. Repeat behind.

14 Squash the flap up. Repeat behind.

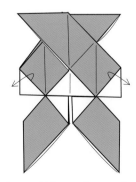

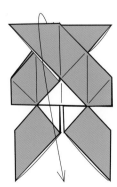

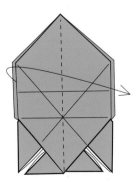

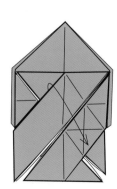

15 Wrap a layer of paper around each side. Repeat behind.

16 Swing the central flap down, all the way. Repeat behind.

17 Swing one layer to the right. Repeat behind.

18 Unsquash the central flap. Repeat behind.

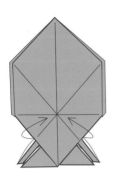

19 Wrap one layer of paper around the central flap on both sides. Repeat behind.

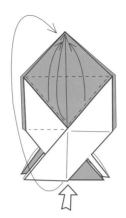

20 Squash the central flap up. Repeat behind.

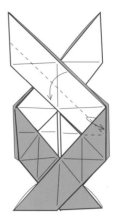

21 Perform a partial squash fold on the central flap, much like you did in step 8. Repeat behind.

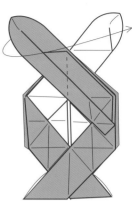

22 Swing the central flap over. Repeat behind.

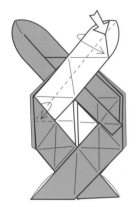

23 Repeat step 21 on this side (still repeating behind).

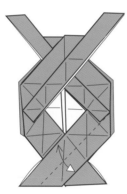

24 Valley fold the bottom flap, and then unfold.

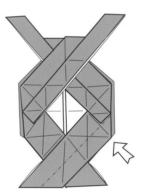

25 Open sink half of the bottom flap. The model will definitely not lie flat.

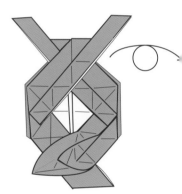

26 Flip the model over, bringing the three-dimensional flap under, so that you are able to work on it on the other side.

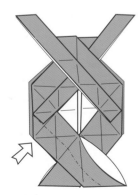

27 Repeat step 25 on this side, completing the complex sink fold.

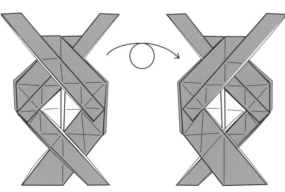

28 Flip the model over.

29 Repeat steps 24–28 on this side.

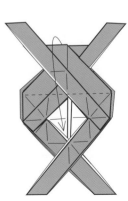

30 Valley fold the top flap, swinging it down.

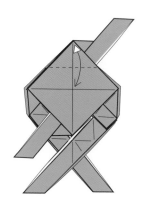

31 Valley fold the top of the central flap, and then unfold.

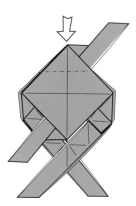

32 Open sink the central flap, using the creases you made in step 31.

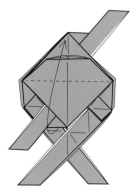

33 Swing the central flap back up.

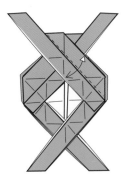

34 Valley fold the right side of the flap down, and then unfold.

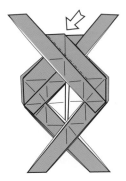

35 Perform a partial closed sink fold on the top of the flap, using the top part of the crease you made in step 34. The model will not lie flat.

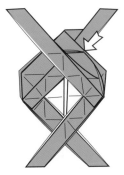

36 Perform an open sink fold on the flap behind the three-dimensional one, completing the complex sink you began in step 35.

37 Perform a valley fold in the center, swinging the central flap over to the right. The model will not lie flat.

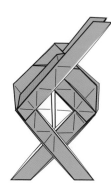

38 Repeat steps 34–36 on the other side.

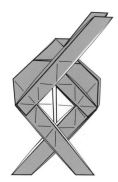

39 Repeat steps 34–37 behind.

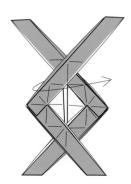

40 Perform a "minor miracle" on the model.

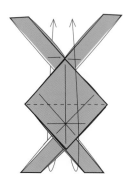

41 Valley fold the central flap up. Repeat behind.

42 Pre-crease a squash fold, using the edges of the white triangle as landmarks. Valley fold and then unfold. Repeat behind.

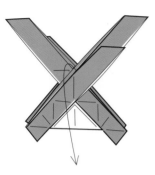

43 Unfold the model back to step 41. Repeat behind.

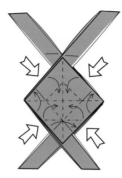

44 Perform a complex squash fold where you sink in all four sides of the creases you made in step 42, while bringing the flap that that forms down. Repeat behind.

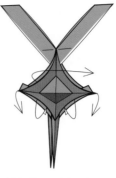

45 One side shown in progress. Perform a "minor miracle" while folding.

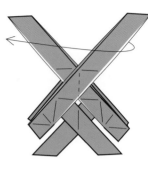

46 Perform a "minor miracle" on the top two flaps.

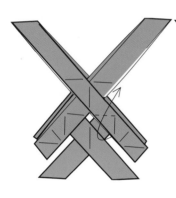

47 Swing up the right flap on each side, using valley folds. Repeat behind.

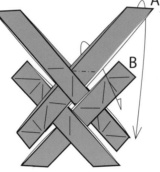

48 Mountain fold the top, right flap down, swinging flap A in front of flap B.

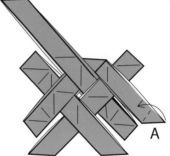

49 Perform a slight valley fold on the bottom of flap A.

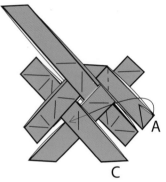

50 Valley fold flap A, tucking it into flap C.

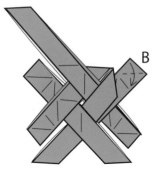

51 Perform a slight valley fold on the top of flap B.

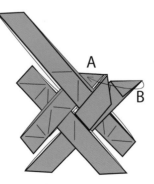

52 Valley fold flap B, tucking it into flap A's pocket.

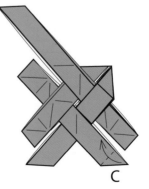

53 Perform a slight valley fold on the bottom of flap C.

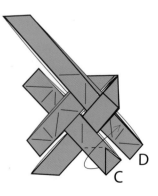

54 Valley fold flap C, tucking it into flap D.

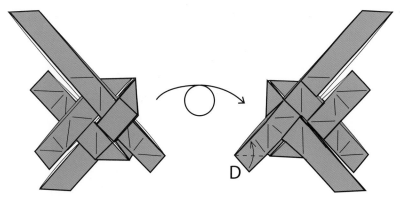

55 Flip the model over.

56 Perform a slight valley fold on the bottom of flap D.

57 Valley fold flap D, tucking it into flap C.

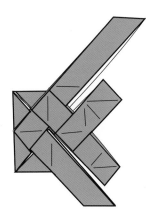

58 Repeat steps 48–57.

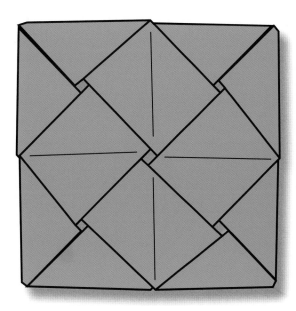

The completed model!

WHEN PIGS FLY!

The name and design for this model is, of course, in reference to the old adage—expressing the belief that a particular notion is so outlandish, that pigs must be flying. Well, pigs are now flying (at least out of paper), and this model is not even as complicated as it looks. The base might be relatively difficult, but from there it is virtually all color changes and technical shaping. This model starts with a bird base, and then develops accordingly from there. It truly is a fun model to fold, so enjoy!

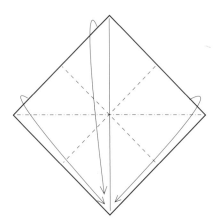

1 Recommended paper: a 10-inch square. Collapse the model into a preliminary base.

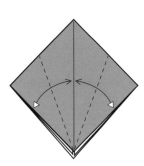

2 Valley fold the two raw edges into the center. Unfold. Repeat behind.

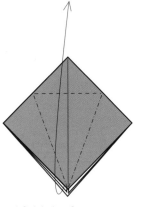

3 Petal fold the flap up, using the creases you just made as guidelines; in doing so, you will form half a bird base. Do not repeat behind.

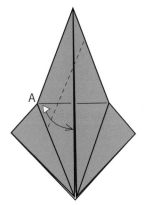

4 Valley fold point A down to the center. Unfold.

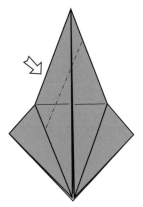

5 Open sink the flap down using the crease made in step 4.

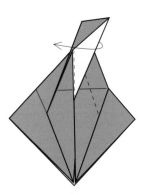

6 Valley fold the white section, swinging the flap over, and, in doing so, valley folding the right edge down.

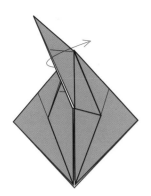

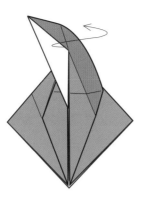

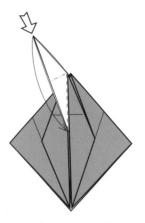

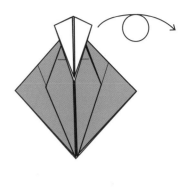

7 Pull the top layer up, opening up a pocket.

8 Repeat step 5 on this side.

9 Collapse the white flap down so that the top corner lies even with the bottom of the white flap.

10 Flip the model over.

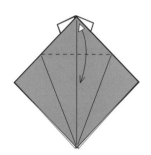

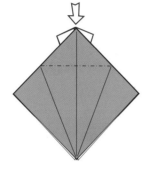

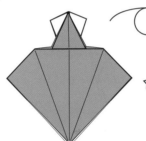

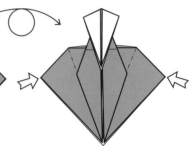

11 Valley fold the top flap down as far as it can go. Unfold.

12 Closed sink the top flap down using the crease you made in step 11 as a guideline.

13 Flip the model over.

14 Inside reverse fold the two sides into the center.

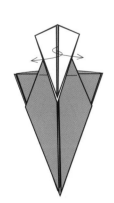

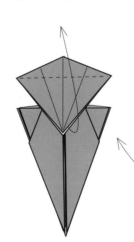

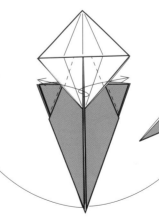

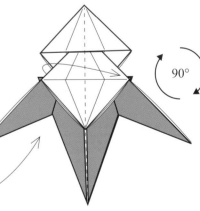

15 Wrap one layer around each side, then collapse them down.

16 Valley fold the corner up as far as it will go.

17 Spread the two tips at the bottom center of the model apart, valley folding them up, while opening up the middle of the model.

18 Valley fold the model in half.

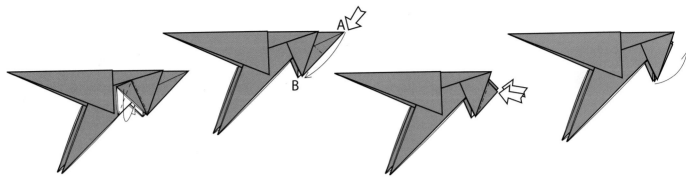

19 Reverse fold the flap under. Repeat behind.

20 Inside reverse fold point A down to the point B.

21 Reverse fold both back flaps in.

22 Reverse fold the flap that will be the tail. As the landmarks are not visible in this diagram, gauge it yourself.

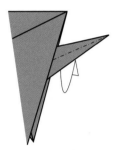

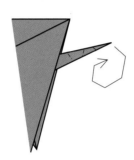

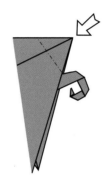

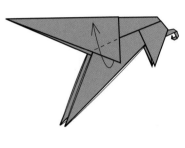

23 Mountain fold the excess tail flap under. Repeat behind.

24 Using a series of reverse folds, curl the tail into the shape of a pig's tail.

25 Inside reverse fold the corner of the model into itself.

26 Valley fold the central flap up. Repeat behind.

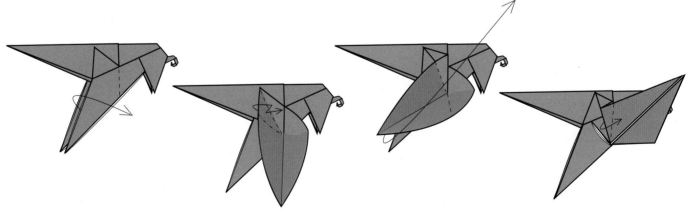

27 Open up the pocket that will be the leg. The model will not lie flat.

28 Pivot fold the leg/wing flap from its top point and another point on the left edge (see next step for details).

29 Collapse the flap up so that the left edge lies even with the edge you made in step 28.

30 Valley fold the flap over as far as it will go.

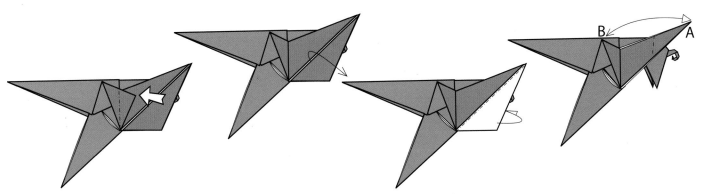

31 Inside reverse fold the flap inside the pocket.

32 Wrap one layer of paper around the leg/wing flap.

33 Mountain fold the white section of the flap behind.

34 Valley fold point A to point B. Unfold.

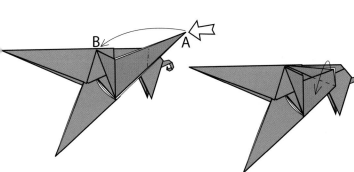

35 Inside reverse fold point A to point B.

36 Valley fold one layer down as far as it will go.

37 Wrap one layer of paper around the wing layer.

38 Valley fold the right edge of the flap to lie even with ear flap's edge, swinging over the wing and pulling out a layer of paper from under the flap.

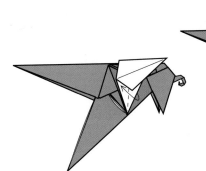

39 Valley fold the right edge of the wing flap over to lie even with its left side, swinging it underneath the wing.

40 Pull out one layer of paper from under the leg flap, while valley folding the wing up.

41 Valley fold the loose layer of paper over to the right side of the leg flap. Then, swing the wing flap back down.

42 Swing the wing/leg flap back over, to the position it was in back in step 38.

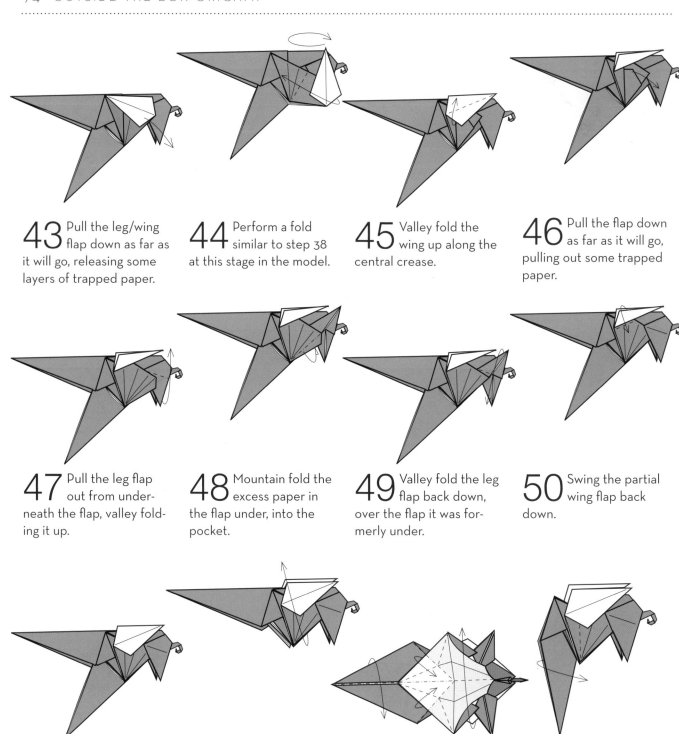

43 Pull the leg/wing flap down as far as it will go, releasing some layers of trapped paper.

44 Perform a fold similar to step 38 at this stage in the model.

45 Valley fold the wing up along the central crease.

46 Pull the flap down as far as it will go, pulling out some trapped paper.

47 Pull the leg flap out from underneath the flap, valley folding it up.

48 Mountain fold the excess paper in the flap under, into the pocket.

49 Valley fold the leg flap back down, over the flap it was formerly under.

50 Swing the partial wing flap back down.

51 Repeat steps 27–50 on the other side.

52 Partially open the model up down the center. The model will not lie flat.

53 Fold the model back in half; in doing so, reverse the left half of the model at the indicated creases and also reverse fold two sections of the reversed area inside of the large reverse fold.

54 Open up the flap that will become the head and ears.

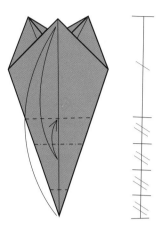

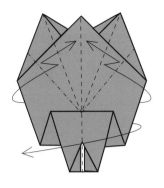

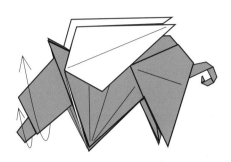

55 (Only the opened head flap is shown.) Perform two valley folds and a mountain fold at $1/2$, $3/8$, and $1/8$ marks respectively, from top to bottom, forming the snout.

56 (Only the opened head flap is shown.) Pivot fold the two sides in at the tips of the ears, while valley folding the head in half.

57 Pull the head flap up, then pull the snout flap up.

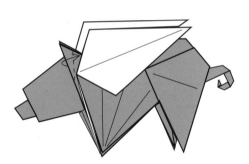

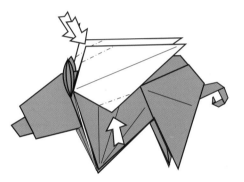

58 Open up the ear, spreading the layers apart. The model will not lie flat. Repeat behind.

59 Closed sink two corners of the wings, slimming them. Repeat behind.

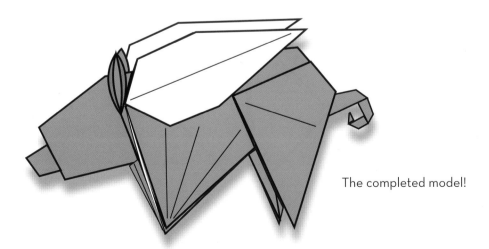

The completed model!

SNOWFLAKE

I designed this model in an attempt to make an interesting floral design that is made out of a square, not a hexagon. Though a true snowflake has six points, this has eight; nevertheless, it is very fun to make and equally fun to admire. The snowflake is probably one of my favorite creations: I am rarely able to replicate the symmetry that is employed in this model!

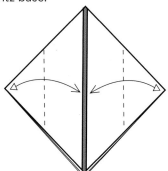

1 Recommended paper: a 10-inch square. Start color side up. Valley fold the four corners of the model into the center, forming a blintz base.

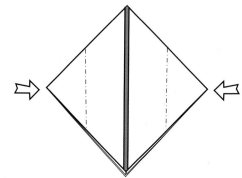

2 Flip the model over.

3 Squash the model into a preliminary base.

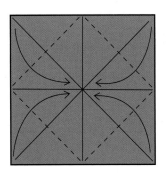

4 Fold the two outside corners into the center. Unfold. Repeat behind.

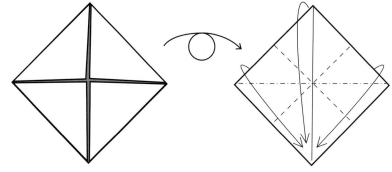

5 Inside reverse-fold those two flaps, along the creases you just made. Repeat behind.

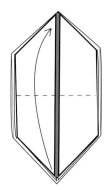

6 Valley fold the bottom flap up to lie even with the top point of the model. Repeat on the other three sides.

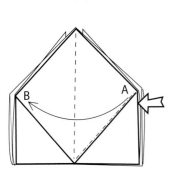

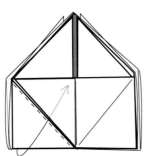

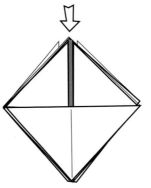

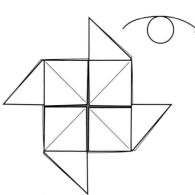

7 Squash point A over to point B. Repeat the process on the other three sides.

8 Put one of the triangular flaps inside of the pocket. Repeat on the other three sides.

9 Squash the central triangular part of the model, while spreading the four other flaps in the same way.

10 Flip the model over.

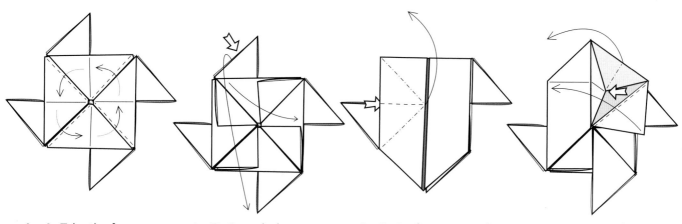

11 Take the four triangular flaps out of their pockets.

12 Squash down one of the triangular flaps, flattening it out.

13 Perform a partial squash on the top flap, bringing it up. The model will not lie flat.

14 Continue the squash fold you began in step 13. In doing so, swing the triangular flap over to lie even with the other flap.

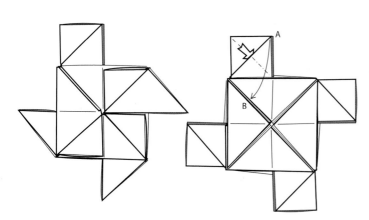

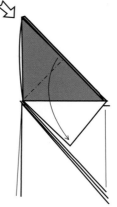

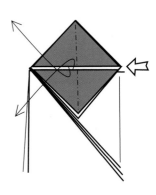

15 Repeat steps 12–14 on the other three flaps.

16 Squash point A down to point B. Repeat behind.

17 Squash the triangular flap down and across.

18 Squash the flap down.

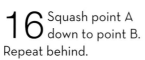

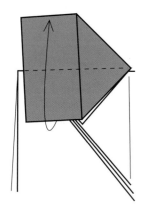

19 Swing the flap back up.

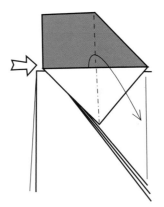

20 Begin to squash the flap down.

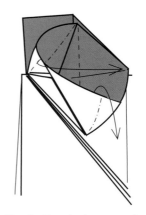

21 Finish the squash fold you started in step 20.

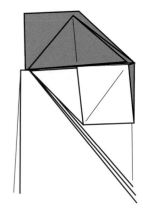

22 Repeat steps 20–21 behind.

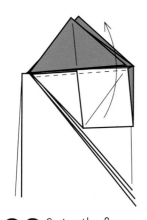

23 Swing the flap up. Repeat behind.

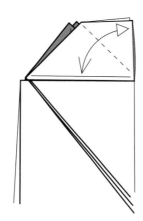

24 Valley fold and unfold. Repeat behind.

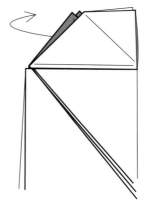

25 Pull out the central part of the colored triangular flap.

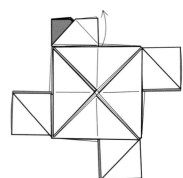

26 Pull out some trapped paper.

27 Valley fold the flap down.

28 Squash the flap down.

29 Flip the model over.

30 Squash the flap across.

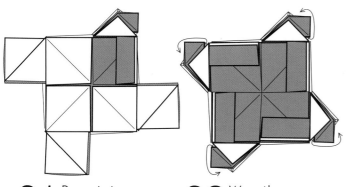

31 Repeat steps 16–30 on the other three flaps.

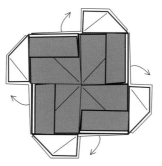

32 Wrap the paper around the colored flaps on all four sides.

33 Bring up a single flap from behind, from each of the four sides.

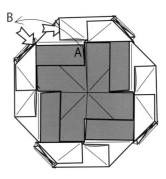

34 Bring point A up to point B by reversing several creases.

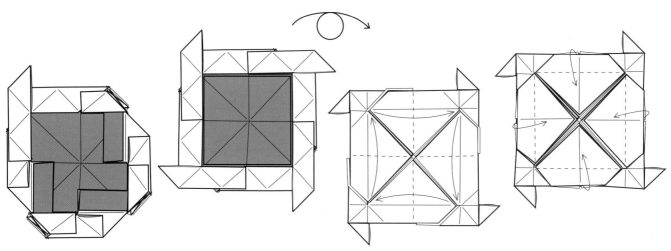

35 Repeat step 34 on the other three sides of the model.

36 Flip the model over.

37 Swing all of the central flaps over one layer, so that they lie symmetrically.

38 Valley fold the top layers on all four of the central flaps.

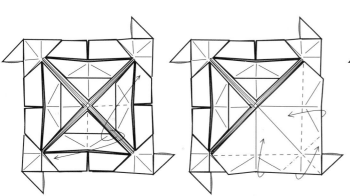
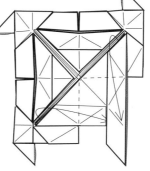
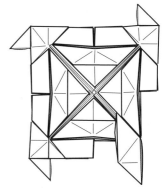

39 Swing the two flaps of one corner apart.

40 Squash the border layer in.

41 Swing the flaps you swung out in step 39 back in.

42 Repeat steps 39–41 on the other three flaps.

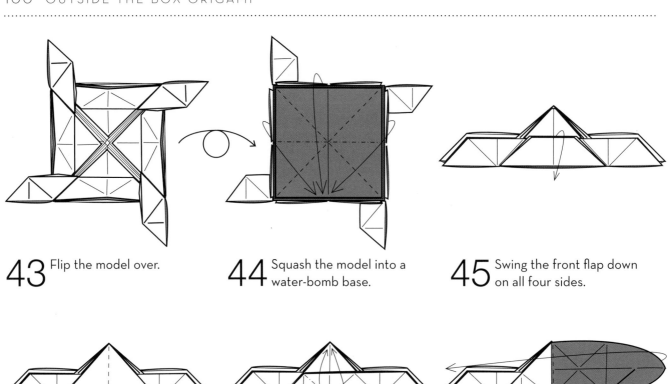

43 Flip the model over.

44 Squash the model into a water-bomb base.

45 Swing the front flap down on all four sides.

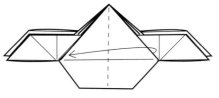

46 Swing one layer to the side.

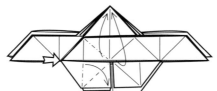

47 Perform a two-part squash fold. The model will not lie flat.

48 Swing the three-dimensional flap over.

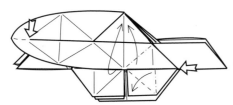

49 Repeat step 47 on the opposite side of the same flap, completing the squash fold.

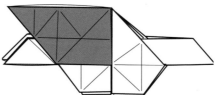

50 Repeat steps 46–49 on the other three sides of the model.

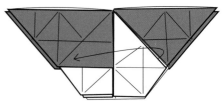

51 Swing one flap over on all sides.

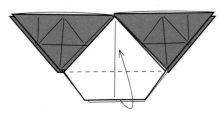

52 Valley fold the bottom of the flap up on all four sides.

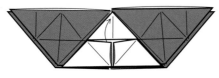

53 Pull out a little bit of paper on each of the four sides.

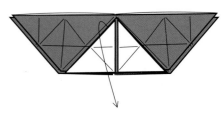

54 Swing the central flap back down to its position in step 52 on all four sides.

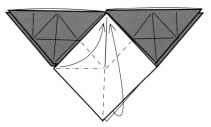

55 Squash the central flap up.

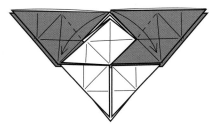

56 Pull out one layer of paper on each side of the central flap.

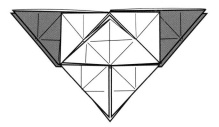

57 Repeat steps 55 and 56 on the other three sides.

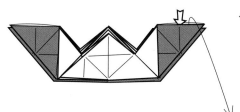

58 Pull out some paper on one of the colored side flaps and squash it back down, using creases you already made.

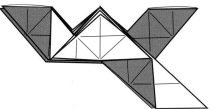

59 Repeat step 58 on the other three sides.

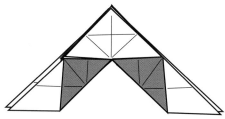

60 Spread the model apart.

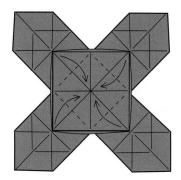

61 Blintz fold the central square.

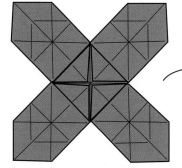

62 Flip the model over.

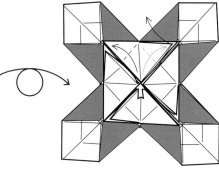

63 Pull one of the central points up, as far as it will go, squashing it down, away from the center.

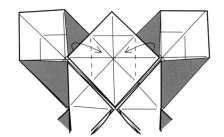

64 Valley fold the two side points into the center.

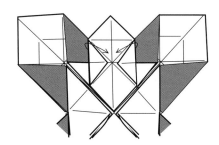

65 Wrap some paper around the central flap.

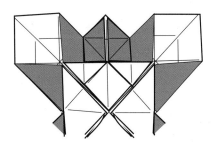

66 Repeat steps 63–65 on the other three sides.

67 Flip the model over.

68 Unsink some paper from the center of the model, on all four sides.

69 Flip the model over.

70 Valley fold the four central flaps away from the center.

71 Unsink some paper into the center of the model, on all four sides.

72 Flip the model over.

73 Mountain fold the four central flaps behind.

74 Swing the four central flaps down.

75 On one of the flaps, valley fold the sides in, so that they are almost touching the center. Unfold.

76 Closed sink the two sides of the flap, using the creases you just made.

77 Flip the model over.

78 Squash the top of the flap down.

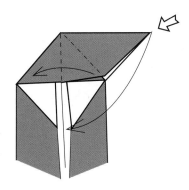

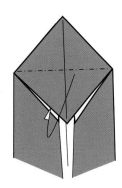

79 Squash the top of that flap into half of a preliminary base.

80 Mountain fold the tip under, locking the flap.

81 Flip the model over.

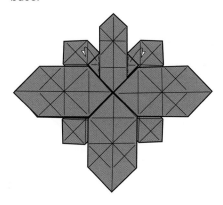

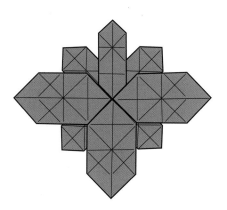

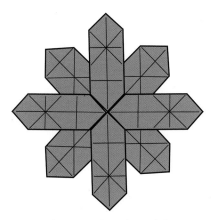

82 Mountain fold the two triangular flaps into their respective pockets.

83 Repeat steps 75–82 on the other three flaps.

The completed model!

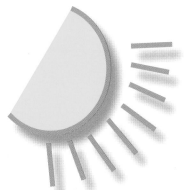

For an interesting effect, hold the snowflake up to the light.

FOLDING OUTSIDE THE BOX

The title of this model is playing to the old adage "thinking outside the box," with the word "thinking" naturally changed to "folding" because of origami. This model was a purposeful paradox, kind of like an M. C. Escher drawing. The enigmatic piece portrays an impossibility which is rendered in the form of an impressive origami model. It is actually far simpler than it looks, but in order for the model to look good, it takes no small amount of technical shaping. The model is done by making three long flaps protrude out of a square base. The base is later collapsed into the box, and two of the long flaps become the arms, and the central flap becomes the piece of paper that the hands are folding. It works best folded out of foil (or wet folded, if you can). Give it a try!

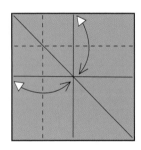

1 Recommended paper: a 12-inch square (minimum). Start color side up. Valley fold two adjacent sides into their respective central creases. Unfold.

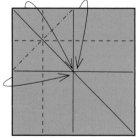

2 Collapse two of the adjacent sides into the center using the creases you made in step 1.

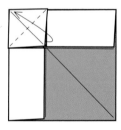

3 Valley fold the corner up to the top left tip.

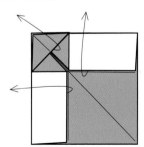

4 Unfold the model back except for the last fold that you made in step 3.

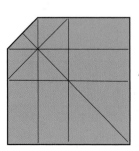

5 Flip the model over.

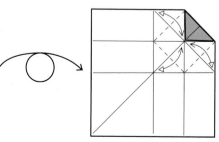

6 Make three valley folds, forming a square of creases (including the upper right edge). Unfold.

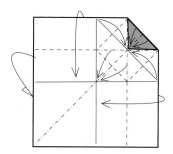

7 Collapse the model using creases you made in previous steps. See the next step for details.

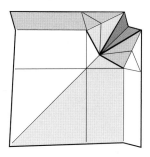

8 Continue collapsing the model.

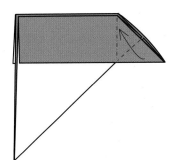

9 Bring the right corner up and over, so that all of those layers lie between the front and back layers.

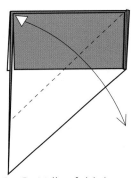

10 Valley fold the top left corner down so that the top edge lies even with the right edge. Unfold. Repeat behind.

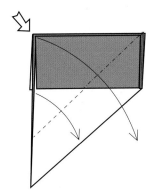

11 Squash the top left corner down and across. Repeat behind.

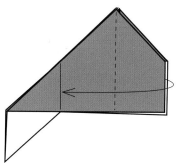

12 Valley fold the right side over to the indicated crease. Repeat behind.

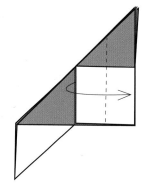

13 Valley fold the right side of the top layer over to the left side. Repeat behind.

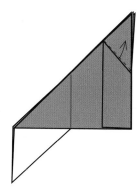

14 Pull out a layer of paper and collapse it down. Repeat behind.

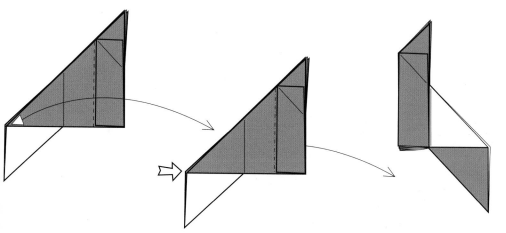

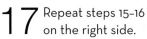

15 Valley fold the left side over, creasing along the edge of the top layer. Unfold.

16 Perform an inside reverse fold using the crease you made in step 15.

17 Repeat steps 15–16 on the right side.

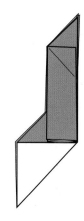

18 Repeat steps 15–16 on the left side.

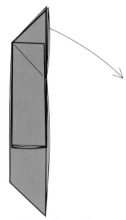

19 Pull out the trapped paper in the top pocket of the model.

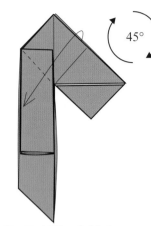

20 Valley fold the top layer of the top section down, opening up what will be the base of the box.

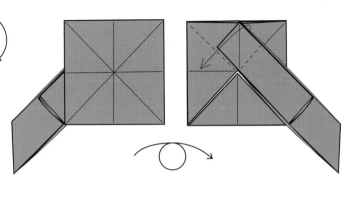

21 Flip the model over.

22 Swing the top left flap down. The model will not lie flat.

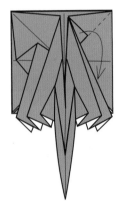

23 Repeat step 22 on the other side.

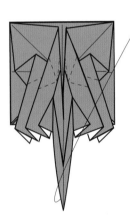

24 Swing the long flap up, squashing the flaps collected at the center apart evenly.

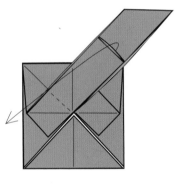

25 Swing the flaps down, separating the layers. The model will not lie flat.

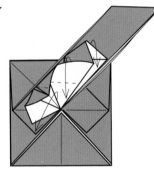

26 Collapse the flap down, so that the model will lie flat. See the next step for details.

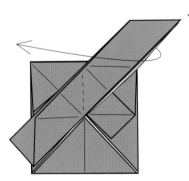

27 Swing the protruding flap over.

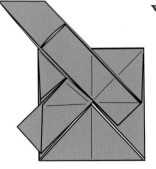

28 Repeat steps 25 and 26 on this side.

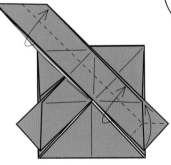

29 Valley fold the top layer up to the edge, collapsing the bottom corner up.

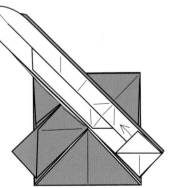

30 Pull out a layer from the pocket and collapse it up.

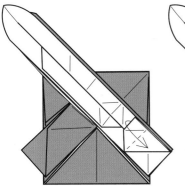

31 Valley fold the flap you just pulled out back down.

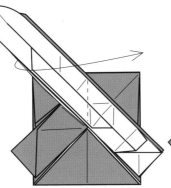

32 Valley fold down the center of the white flap, swinging it across.

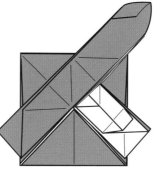

33 Repeat steps 29-31 on the other side.

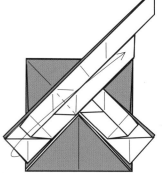

34 Valley fold the bottom left flap up as far as it will go.

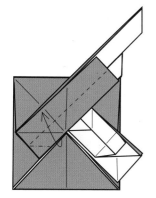

35 Collapse the flap up, valley folding the raw edge to the top.

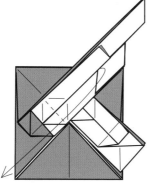

36 Valley fold the flap back down, swinging it to its former position.

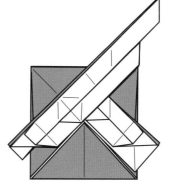

37 Repeat steps 34-36 on the other side.

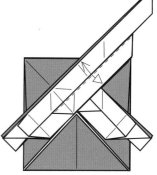

38 Valley fold the top flap up as far as it will go, along the edge of the top layer. Unfold.

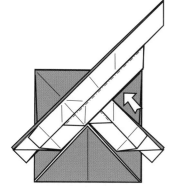

39 Open sink the flap inside, using the crease you made in step 38.

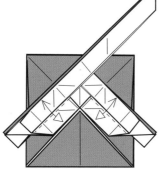

40 Valley fold the two flaps up to their edge, in the same way that you did in step 38. Then unfold.

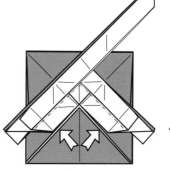

41 Open sink the two flaps in, using the creases you made in step 40.

42 Pull out some paper from each side of the two flaps and collapse it down. See next step for details.

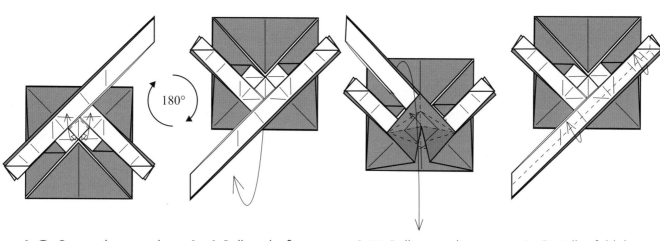

43 Crease the central layer up at its edges, as far as it will go. Unfold.

44 Pull up the flap, opening the bottom pocket of the model.

45 Pull up one layer of paper within the opened pocket. Then, collapsing the center of that area, squash the top flap back down.

46 Valley fold the flap up to its edge, collapsing the corner accordingly.

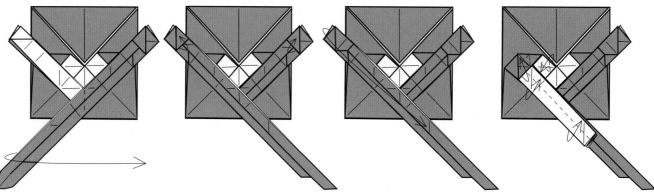

47 Repeat step 46 on the other side, swinging the central flap over.

48 Pull out a layer of paper from the pocket on each side, valley folding it back down.

49 Valley fold the top left tip of the flap down.

50 Collapse the model as shown. See next step for details.

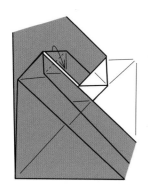
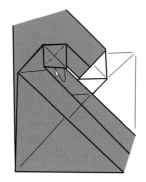
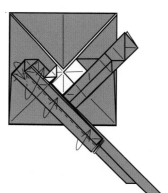
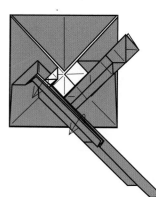

51 Valley fold the flap down.

52 Reverse fold the flap under and inside, into the pocket.

53 Collapse the model as shown, valley folding the flap up to the edge.

54 Swing the layer down as if valley folding it. Do not entirely undo the fold you made in step 53.

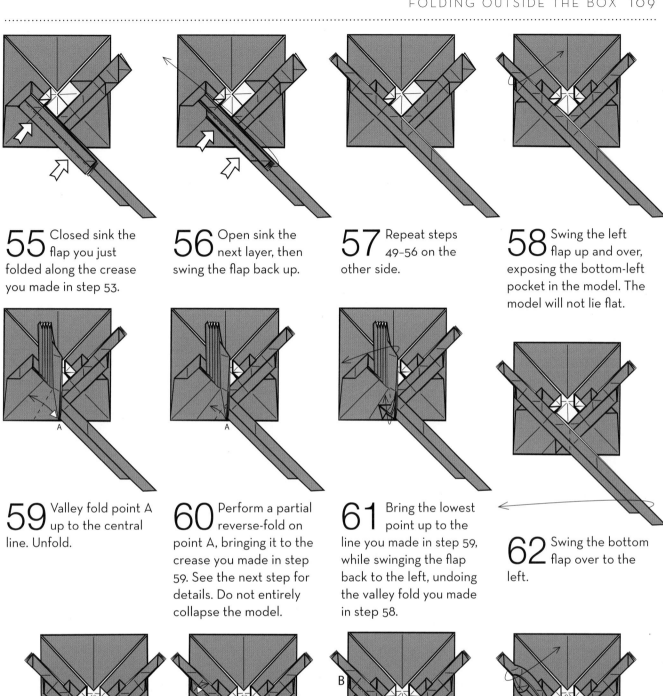

55 Closed sink the flap you just folded along the crease you made in step 53.

56 Open sink the next layer, then swing the flap back up.

57 Repeat steps 49–56 on the other side.

58 Swing the left flap up and over, exposing the bottom-left pocket in the model. The model will not lie flat.

59 Valley fold point A up to the central line. Unfold.

60 Perform a partial reverse-fold on point A, bringing it to the crease you made in step 59. See the next step for details. Do not entirely collapse the model.

61 Bring the lowest point up to the line you made in step 59, while swinging the flap back to the left, undoing the valley fold you made in step 58.

62 Swing the bottom flap over to the left.

63 Repeat steps 58–62 on this side.

64 Valley fold the left edge of the central flap up to the top. Unfold. Crease through all layers but the bottom one.

65 Open sink the lower side into the upper half of the flap. This sink will not go all the way from point B to point C. The model will not lie flat.

66 Swing the left flap up and over, exposing the bottom-left pocket in the model.

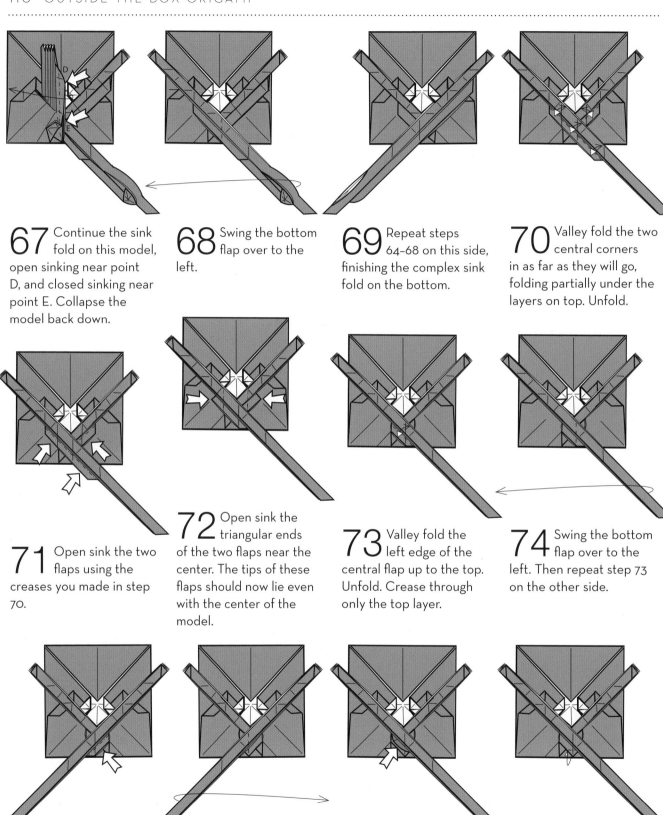

67 Continue the sink fold on this model, open sinking near point D, and closed sinking near point E. Collapse the model back down.

68 Swing the bottom flap over to the left.

69 Repeat steps 64–68 on this side, finishing the complex sink fold on the bottom.

70 Valley fold the two central corners in as far as they will go, folding partially under the layers on top. Unfold.

71 Open sink the two flaps using the creases you made in step 70.

72 Open sink the triangular ends of the two flaps near the center. The tips of these flaps should now lie even with the center of the model.

73 Valley fold the left edge of the central flap up to the top. Unfold. Crease through only the top layer.

74 Swing the bottom flap over to the left. Then repeat step 73 on the other side.

75 Sink the flap using the crease you made in step 74. You will open sink the top of the flap, and closed sink the bottom.

76 Swing the flap back over as far as you can. The model will not lie flat.

77 Repeat step 75 on this side, finishing the sink you started in step 75.

78 Mountain fold the tip of the flap behind.

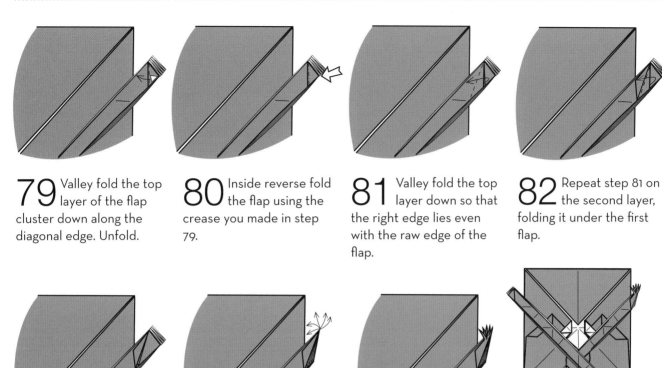

79 Valley fold the top layer of the flap cluster down along the diagonal edge. Unfold.

80 Inside reverse fold the flap using the crease you made in step 79.

81 Valley fold the top layer down so that the right edge lies even with the raw edge of the flap.

82 Repeat step 81 on the second layer, folding it under the first flap.

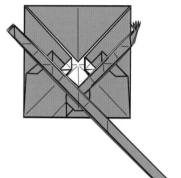

83 Repeat steps 79–82 on the remaining three flaps.

84 Pull the layers apart, forming the five points into the fingers of the hand. See next step for details.

85 This is how the hand should look.

86 Repeat steps 79–85 on the other side.

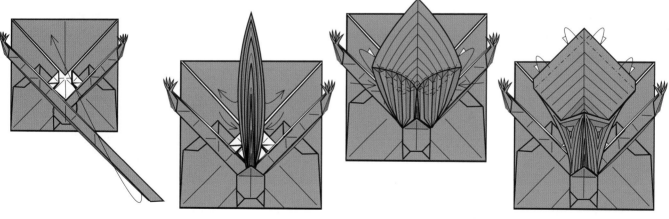

87 Swing the center flap up. The model will no longer lie flat.

88 Spread the top layers of the central flap while pinching the central ones into the center, making sure that they don't spread.

89 Collapse the top face down while pleating the area beneath.

90 Mountain fold the two edges in and under along the first crease from the top edges.

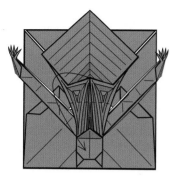

91 Bring the square face down (it will become the sheet of paper coming out of the box). It should appear to be a square floating out of nowhere (the supporting flap should disappear behind the square when you look at it from the front). See next step for details.

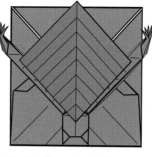

92 For simplicity's sake, the next steps do not show the square or arms and hands on top.

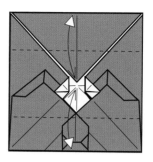

93 Valley fold the top and bottom edges into the center. Unfold.

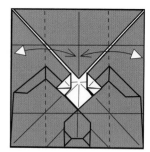

94 Repeat step 93 on the right and left sides.

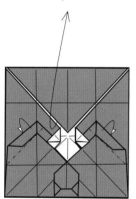

95 Pull the top flap up, while mountain folding the two flaps behind.

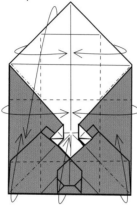

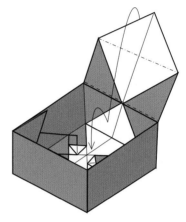

96 Collapse the model using the creases you made in the previous several steps.

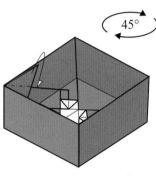

97 Valley fold the flap down, mountain folding the top of it so that it lies even with the side and bottom of the box.

98 Mountain fold the triangular flaps along the side into their respective pockets (including the one you can't see in this image).

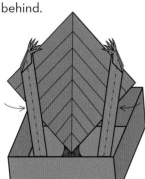

99 (The arms and paper are now shown.) Pinch the arms, making them more three-dimensional.

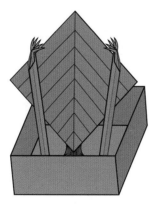

100 Shape to taste, making the arms look more organic.

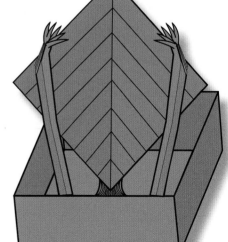

The completed model!